Uganda:
The Land and Its People

Godfrey Mwakikagile

Uganda: The Land and Its People
Godfrey Mwakikagile

First Edition

ISBN 978-9987-9308-9-0

New Africa Press
Dar es Salaam, Tanzania

3

Introduction

THIS is an abridged version of my other work on Uganda. It's a general introduction to Uganda as a country and as a nation.

It serves as a broad introduction for a number of reasons.

It's intended to introduce Uganda to people who know nothing or very little about this East African country. It provides basic information which even some people who already know about Uganda may find to be useful. It also contains some information which may be helpful even to experts in the field.

It can also help tourists and other people going to Uganda for different reasons, for example, as relief workers, as missionaries, as businessmen or simply as travellers just passing through.

Many people go to Uganda to do research in different fields. Others go there just to live. And they all may find this work to be useful.

But it's not written as a scholarly work even if some people may find it to be useful in their scholarly pursuits. It's written simply as a general book which can help different people who want to learn a few things about Uganda in different fields such as history, politics, social and cultural studies, economics and others.

It may even encourage some of them to learn more about this magnificent land which is also known as "the pearl of Africa" in the tropics. In fact, the equator runs right through Uganda.

I have covered different subjects which, I believe, should be enough to provide basic information about Uganda to anybody who wants to get a general picture of the country.

Subjects covered include geography, history, different cultures and ethnic groups which collectively constitute the nation.

If this work can help even just one person to learn a few things about Uganda, it will have achieved its purpose.

And as an African, I feel that it's my duty to help foreigners learn a few important things about one of the African countries I have decided to write about as my contribution towards a better understanding of our continent.

Welcome to Uganda, and welcome to Africa.

Part One:

The Land

UGANDA is divided into four administrative regions: Northern, Eastern, Central and Western. It's also divided into districts, counties and sub-counties.

Regions are divided into districts. There are 80 districts. Districts are subdivided into counties or sub-districts, and counties into sub-counties. Sub-counties are divided into parishes, and parishes into villages.

Most districts are named after their main commercial and administrative towns.

The largest region in terms of area is the Northern region. It has an area of 85,392 square kilometres. But it has the smallest population. In 2008, it had a population of 6,652,300.

The second-largest is the Central Region with an area of 61,403 square kilometres. It also has the largest population and had 7,750,600 people in 2008.

The Western Region is the third-largest with an area of 55,277 square kilometres. Its population also is the third-largest in the country. The region had a population of 7,497,300 in 2008.

The Eastern Region is the smallest. It has an area of 39,479 square kilometres. But its population is the second-largest. In 2008, the region had a population of 7,692,500, a close second to that of the Central Region.

The Central Region also has the largest number of the principal towns and cities in the country: Kampala, Kira, Nansana, Masaka, and Entebbe.

There are also many other towns in Uganda in all the provinces with populations of more than 10,000.

There are also five traditional Bantu kingdoms which have existed since pre-colonial times. Although they were stripped much of their power after independence, they now enjoy limited autonomy mainly in the cultural sphere. The kingdoms are Buganda, Bunyoro, Toro, Ankole and Busoga.

The kingdoms played an important role in the history of the region before the advent of colonial rule and constituted the nucleus of colonial Uganda. They were also among the most prominent traditional institutions – on the entire continent – which predated colonialism.

Buganda was the most well-known in Uganda. It was not the oldest but it became the most powerful kingdom in the region. And when the British established the Uganda Protectorate, the Buganda kingdom constituted the nucleus of the colonial territory. Today Buganda is the largest of the traditional kingdoms in the country. It's bordered by Lake Victoria on the south.

It was originally a vassal state of Bunyoro but rapidly grew in power in the 18th and 19th centuries, eclipsing its former ruler, Bunyoro, the neighbouring kingdom to the west. It also seized territory held by Bunyoro and dominated other areas.

After the British established a protectorate, they used

the Buganda kingdom for administrative purposes. The kingdom was allowed to exercise some control over the other kingdoms – Toro, Ankole and Busoga – and many Gandas became administrators in other parts of the protectorate.

The Baganda also took advantage of the education provided by the colonial rulers and by the missionaries and they became the most educated people in Uganda. And the highest institution of learning in Uganda and in the entire East Africa, Makerere University College, was built by the British in the Buganda kingdom. It also became the most prestigious academic institution throughout black Africa and had students from as far away as Ghana, Nigeria and southern Africa.

The Buganda kingdom became so influential that the colonial history of Uganda was in many ways written from the perspective of the Baganda., A disproportionately large number of them not only worked as civil servants in many parts of Uganda but were also the primary contact with the colonial rulers in the native population. And when the country won independence in 1962, the Buganda kingdom had the highest standard of living in Uganda. It also had the highest literacy rate in the entire East Africa.

But independence also led to fundamental changes in the distribution of power, weakening the kingdom. And even before independence, there were warning signs that such changes would come with the end of colonial rule. A number of political parties were formed as independence approached and were ready to contest for power, encouraged by the prospect of elections allowed by the colonial rulers.

The rulers of the Buganda kingdom were apprehensive of the situation because they realised that elections would lead to fundamental changes in power. The centre of power would be at the national level and power of the traditional rulers would be weakened considerably.

There was even wider opposition to such changes

9

when the secretary of state for colonies said in a speech in London in 1953 that there was a possibility of a federation of the three East African territories – Kenya, Uganda and Tanganyika, all ruled Britain – similar to that of central Africa which was known as the Federation of Rhodesia and Nyasaland.

Also known as the Central African Federation, it was composed of Southern Rhodesia (now Zimbabwe) which was the centre of power, Northern Rhodesia (Zambia today) and Nyasaland (renamed Malawi).

Many Ugandans, not just the Baganda in the Buganda kingdom, were aware of that federation. They also knew that it was dominated by whites. Therefore supporting formation of an East African federation in which the interests of the white settlers would be paramount was totally out of the question.

Ugandans – and the people of Tanganyika as well as Kenya – feared that the federation would be dominated by the racist settlers of Kenya which was then in the midst of the Mau Mau uprising. In fact, Ugandans and other East Africans in Kenya and Tanganyika had resisted a similar suggestion in the 1930s.

The situation got even worse for the Baganda when the colonial governor of Uganda, Andrew Cohen, said the Buganda kingdom's special status would have to be sacrificed in the interests of a new and larger nation-state which would wield central authority for the entire country of Uganda.

The kabaka of the Buganda kingdom, Edward Frederick Mutesa, refused to cooperate with the governor. He did not want his kingdom to be integrated with the rest of Uganda and demanded that Buganda should be separated from the rest of the protectorate. The governor responded by sending the kabaka into a comfortable exile in London.

But the kabaka's forced departure had unintended consequences. He became a hero among his people,

10

fuelling separatist and anti-colonial sentiments in the Buganda kingdom. The governor could not find anyone in the kingdom who was prepared or able to support his plan of centralising power at the national level. And after two frustrating years of unrelenting hostility and obstruction to his plan among the Banganda, he was forced to reinstate the kabaka.

In return, the governor secured the kabaka's agreement not to oppose independence within the larger Uganda framework. But a number of conservative Bagandans who were fiercely loyal to Buganda as a kingdom were willing to support inclusion of the kingdom in the new nation of Uganda only if Uganda was headed by the kabaka.

But there were some Baganda who were opposed to that. These were mainly Catholics who felt that they had been excluded from the establishment in Buganda which was dominated by Protestants. They went on to form their own political party, the Democratic Party (DP), under the leadership of Benedicto Kiwanuka.

The situation was not peculiar to Buganda. Religion and politics were equally inseparable in the other kingdoms and in other parts of the country.

The Democratic Party had other supporters besides Catholics and was probably the best organized of all the parties preparing for elections before independence.

Elsewhere in Uganda, the emergence of the kabaka as a political force provoked immediate hostility. Political parties and local interest groups were riddled with divisions and rivalries but they shared one concern: they were determined not to be dominated by Buganda.

In 1960 a political organiser, Milton Obote, from Lango in the northern-central part of the country, seized the initiative and formed a new party, the Uganda People's Congress (UPC) as a coalition of all those outside the Roman Catholic-dominated DP who opposed Buganda hegemony.

His party was not only national in scope but

11

transcended ethnicity and regional loyalties in its leadership and political orientation. It was the first truly national party ever formed in Ugandan history.

But the people of the Buganda kingdom remained a major political force in Ugandan politics. In terms of population, there were too many of them to be overlooked or ignored. But they were also too few to dominate the country as whole.

In 1959, about three years before independence, Buganda's population was 2 million out of Uganda's total of 6 million. Even discounting the many non-Baganda resident in Buganda, there were at least 1 million people who owed allegiance to the kabaka. And they were resolutely opposed to centralisation of power at the national level.

The main objective of modern nationalists like Obote – and of the colonial rulers – was still the establishment of a unitary state. And it was obvious that Buganda autonomy and a strong central government were incompatible.

The British announced that elections would be held in March 1961 for "responsible government," the next-to-last stage of preparation before the formal granting of independence.

It was assumed that those winning the election would gain valuable experience in office, preparing them for the probable responsibility of governing after Uganda emerged from colonial rule.

Kabaka Mutesa urged a total boycott of the election in Buganda kingdom because attempts by the Baganda to secure promises of future autonomy had been rebuffed. The only exception were the Baganda who supported the Democratic Party.

So, when the voters went to the polls throughout Uganda to elect 82 members of the National Assembly (parliament), it was only the Roman Catholic supporters of the Democratic Party in Buganda kingdom who braved severe public pressure and voted, capturing 20 of

Buganda's 21 allotted seats.

The results led to an unusual political development, giving the Democratic Party a majority of seats, although it had a minority of 416,000 votes nationwide versus 495,000 for the Uganda People's Congress.

Benedicto Kiwanuka became the new chief minister of Uganda and served from 2 July 1961 to 1 March 1962. He also became Uganda's first prime minister but served for only two months from 1 March 1962 to 30 April 1962 when he was succeeded by Milton Obote. He was killed by Idi Amin's regime on 22 September 1972.

Buganda separatists were shocked by the election results and formed a party called Kabaka Yekka which means "king only." It was a monarchist political party fiercely loyal to the kabaka but had second thoughts about not participating in the next election.

In 1962 the Kabaka Yekka merged with the Uganda People's Congress and participated in the National Assembly elections, thus gaining influence at the national level.

Before the elections, a British commission had proposed a federal form of government for Uganda and the Kabaka Yekka (KY) quickly accepted the proposal because it suited its interests. According to the recommendations by the commission, Buganda would enjoy a measure of internal autonomy but only if it participated fully in the national government.

For its part, the Uganda People's Congress was equally anxious to eject its Democratic Party rivals from interim administration before they became entrenched.

Obote reached an understanding with Kabaka Mutesa and the Kabaka Yekka, accepting Buganda's special federal relationship and even a provision by which the kabaka could appoint Buganda's representatives to the National Assembly in return for a strategic alliance to defeat the Democratic Partyy.

The kabaka was also promised the largely ceremonial

13

position of head of state of Uganda, which was of great symbolic importance to the Baganda.

This marriage of convenience between the Uganda People's Congress and the Kabaka Yekka made inevitable the defeat of the Democratic Party interim government.

In the aftermath of the April 1962 final election a few months before independence, the national parliament consisted of 43 UPC members, 24 from Kabaka Yekka, and 24 from the Democratic Party.

The new UPC-KY coalition led Uganda to independence on 9 October 1962, with Obote as prime minister and the kabaka as head of state.

However, the monarchy of Buganda and much of its autonomy was revoked, along with that of the other four Ugandan kingdoms, after independence.

The most important question in post-independence Uganda was the role of the Buganda king in national politics because of Buganda's special status and the role the kingdom had played in the history of the country since the advent of colonial rule. He remained a highly influential figure especially among his people, the Baganda, and could not be ignored.

Although there were four kingdoms, the real question was how much control over Buganda the central government should have. The power of the king as a uniting symbol for the Baganda became clear following his forced exile to Britain in 1953. His people rallied behind him. And when negotiations for independence threatened the autonomous status of Buganda, leading figures in the kingdom organised a political party to protect the king.

The issue was successfully presented as a question of survival of the Baganda as a separate nation because the position of the king had been central to Buganda's precolonial culture. On that basis, defence of the kingship attracted overwhelming support in local Buganda government elections which were held just before independence. To oppose the king in Buganda at that time would have meant political suicide.

Kabaka Mutesa was again forced into exile and fled to Britain in May 1966, three years and eight months after the country won independence. He died in London in November 1969. He was 45.

Uganda became a republic in 1967 and kingdoms were abolished.

Obote himself was overthrown by Amin in January 1971.

When Obote regained power in 1980, more than half of all the Baganda had never lived under their king.

The Conservative Party, a marginal group led by the last man who served as Buganda's prime minister under Kabaka Mutesa, contested the 1980 elections but received little support in the former kingdom.

Yet, most of the people in the Buganda kingdom were against Obote. And when Yoweri Museveni launched guerrilla warfare to oust him, he got a lot of support from the Baganda.

Many of them joined his guerrilla army and the insurgency against Obote was conducted entirely in Buganda until its final year, largely fuelled by the hostility most Baganda had towards Obote and the Uganda People's Congress.

Ironically, Obote's wife Miriam was a Ganda from the Buganda kingdom and she became the leader of the Uganda People's Congress after her husband died.

The Buganda kingdom regained some of its former glory under President Museveni, including restoration of kingship. Ronald Mutebi, the son of Kabaka Edward Frederick Mutesa, became king but never had the same power and influence his predecessors had.

He was crowned as the 36th kabaka in 1993 after Museveni reinstated the position of kabaka under a new constitution. But the kabaka's position today is largely symbolic.

The kabaka serves as s*sabataka* – head of the clans and of the cultural kingdom of Buganda, and not as a political and military leader as was the case before.

Buganda is now a constitutional monarchy with a parliament called Lukiiko. But the kabaka attends only two sessions in a year; first when he is opening the first session of the year and, second, when he is closing the last session of the year.

Although Buganda has been the most prominent kingdom in Uganda since colonial times, the other kingdoms have also stood out in their own ways throughout the nation's history and even before then when Uganda did not exist as a single political entity.

Next to Buganda is Bunyoro. It's the oldest kingdom in Uganda and was once the most powerful, militarily and economically, in the Great Lakes region before the advent of colonial rule.

At the peak of its power, Bunyoro controlled almost the entire region between Lake Victoria (where Buganda is located), Lake Edward and Lake Albert. Around 1520, the rulers of Bunyoro even raided the Rwanda area ruled by the Tutsi. The power of Bunyoro then faded until the mid-17th century when a long period of expansion began, with the empire dominating the region by the early 18th century.

Bunyoro rose to power by controlling a number of the holiest shrines in the region, the lucrative Kibiro saltworks of Lake Albert, and having the highest quality of metallurgy in the region. This is what made it the strongest military and economic power in the Great Lakes area.

Bunyoro began to fade in the late 18th century due to internal divisions, paving the way for the rise of Buganda as the most powerful kingdom in the region.

The rulers of Buganda seized Kooki and Budu regions from Bunyoro at the end of the 18th century. And around 1830, the large province of Toro separated from Bunyoro, taking with it many of the lucrative salt works.

And in the south, Rwanda and Nkore (Ankole) were both growing rapidly, taking over some of the smaller kingdoms that had been Bunyoro's vassals.

Thus by the mid-19th century Bunyoro was a far smaller state. But it was still wealthy and controlled lucrative trade routes over Lake Victoria and linking to the coast of the Indian Ocean.

Bunyoro profited especially from the trade in ivory. It was, however, continually imperiled by the now potent Buganda kingdom which wanted to take control of the trade routes for itself.

A long struggle between the two ensued, and both armed themselves with European weapons. Buganda finally emerged as the most powerful kingdom in the region.

When Great Britain declared the area of what is now Uganda a protectorate in 1894, the king of Bunyoro, Omukama Kaberega – Omukama means king – was strongly opposed to the imposition of imperial rule on his territory. Buganda, Bunyoro's rival, supported Great Britain in her effort to seize Bunyoro.

In 1899, King Kabarega was captured and exiled to the Seychelles and Bunyoro became part of the Uganda Protectorate. Seychelles is also the same place where the Asantehene (king) of the Ashanti in the Gold Coast was sent in exile when he resisted British attempts to seize his kingdom.

After Bunyoro was annexed by the British, significant parts of its territory were given to Buganda and Toro kingdoms as punishment for its resistance to imperial rule. Buganda administrators were sent into Bunyoro to help run the kingdom on behalf of the British colonial rulers as they did in much of Uganda.

The Banyoro revolted in 1907 but were suppressed. Relations improved somewhat and the kingdom remained loyal to Great Britain. Bunyoro's loyalty to the imperial power brought some dividends and the kingdom was given more autonomy in 1934. And today it remains a prominent kingdom in Uganda and one of the most well-known traditional political entities in East Africa.

Toro is another major traditional kingdom and which was once part of Bunyoro.

It was established when the eldest son of the king of Bunyoro rebelled against his father's rule and founded his own independent political entity in the kingdom's southern province. Toro was incorporated back into Bunyoro in 1876 but it reasserted its independence in 1891.

The people of the Toro kingdom are known as Batoro, an interlacustrine Bantu-speaking people. Their language is Lutoro and that of the Banyoro – Lunyoro.

They inhabit a high plateau on Uganda's southwestern border between Lake Albert and Lake Edward. The region is bounded by the Ruwenzori Mountains on the west in southwestern Uganda.

In pre-colonial times, the Batoro lived in a highly centralized kingdom like Buganda, which was stratified like the society of Bunyoro.

And throughout its history, the kingdom of Toro had a cattle-owing class, the Hima who are related to another cattle-owing ethnic group the Tutsi of Rwanda and Burundi. And the overwhelming majority of the Toro people, known as Iru, were small-scale farmers.

Traditionally, the Toro society is highly stratified and social classes are very important in the lives of the people. The Bito, formerly a people pastoralist people who are Nilotic and who came from the north, claim greater wealth and privileges than the Iru who are also known as Bairu. So do the Hima.

Therefore, in general, the Iru are lower than the other two in terms of wealth and social status.

The Iru are Bantu and their domination by the Nilotic and other non-Bantu people is a common feature in the history of the Great Lakes region including Rwanda, Burundi and eastern Congo where non-Bantus – who migrated from the north and probably from Ethiopia in the case of the Tutsi – have dominated Bantu-speaking people for centuries.

Crops grown for local consumption include millet, bananas, cassava, and sweet potatoes. And the main cash crops are coffee, cotton and wheat. Fish are another important product.

Toro lands include rain forests, dense bamboo stands, papyrus swamps, plains of elephant grass and shores of Lake Albert and Lake Edward.

The region is also a tourist attraction. Its attractions include a national park and significant numbers of many species including elephants, hippos and antelope.

The kingdom had about 700,000 people at the beginning of the 21st centuty.

And like the other monarchies in Uganda, the Toro kingdom was abolished in 1967 during the presidency of Milton Obote as stipulated in the 1966 constitution. But it was re-instituted in 1993 together with the other traditional kingdoms.

Ankole is another traditional kingdom in Uganda, one of the big four, which has also played an important role in the history of the country. It became a part of the Uganda Protectorate in October 1901.

Also known as Nkore, it's located in southwestern Uganda east of Lake Edward and ceased to exist as an administrative unit during Idi Amin's reign when it was divided into six districts.

Traditionally, it was ruled by a monarch known as Omugabe. The people of Ankole, who are Bantu, are called Banyankole – singular Munyankole – and their language is Lunyankole.

The history of the Ankole kingdom is inextricably linked with the history of the Hima who became the dominant ethnic group after they migrated into the area from the north.

The pastoralist Hima, also known as Bahima, imposed

their rule on the Bairu (Iru) in Ankole as they had done elsewhere in the region where they conquered other Bantu farming groups.

As elsewhere, the Bantu Iru in Ankole were considered to be inferior to the Hima. And the symbol of inequality was cattle ownership. Only the Hima could own catle. The two groups interacted commercially but were separate in terms of identity and social status.

The differences were maintained and reinforced by a number of legal and social restrictions including prohibition of intermarriage between the Hima and the Iru. If such marriage took place, it would be annulled.

Although the Hima became the rulers of Ankole, they were far outnumbered by the Iru. The Iru were also compelled, by custom and tradition, to pay tribute to the Hima who also demanded gifts from them.

The Iru were able to provided that because the Hima population among them was small. So they could afford gifts and tribute demanded by the Hima. And that helped make relations between the two groups tolerable.

Still, the subordinate status of the Iru was also maintained because the Hima had superior military organisation and training which helped to perpetuate their dominant position as the rulers of Ankole.

The kingdom of Ankole under Hima leadership expanded through annexation of territories in the south and in the east. And the rulers continued to enforce social stratification even among the people they conquered.

In many cases, conquered herders were incorporated into the dominant Hima stratum of society. And agricultural populations were adopted as Iru or as slaves and were treated as legally inferior to their conquerors. Also neither group of the conquered could own cattle. Slaves could not even herd cattle owned by the Hima. And only Hima men could serve in the army.

The decision by the Hima to prohibit the Iru from serving in the army and from getting military training had profound implications. It eliminated the threat of Iru rebellion against the rulers.

Iru legal inferiority was manifested best by the legal prohibition against cattle ownership among them. Because marriages were legitimised through the exchange of cattle, this prohibition helped reinforce the ban on Hima-Iru intermarriage.

The Iru were also denied high-level political appointments, although they were often appointed to assist local administrators in Iru villages.

But in spite of all these injustices, the Iru still had a number of ways to redress their grievances against Hima overlords. It's true that they did not have the same power as the Hima because of their legal status as a conquered people who were regarded and treated as inferior. Still, Iru men could petition the king to end unfair treatment by a Hima patron. Also, Iru people could not be subjugated to Hima cattle-owners without entering into a patron-client contract.

Eventually, hegemonic control of the Ankole kingdom by the Hima came to an end for a number of reasons. There were several social developments and pressures which collectively worked to destroy Hima domination of Ankole.

One of the most effective was intermarriage between the Hima and the Iru despite prohibitions against such marriage. The children of these unions often demanded their rights as cattle owners, a demand which often led to feuding and cattle-raiding.

And during the 19th century, groups launched repeated attacks against the Hima. These attacks came from groups which were in an area that is known as Rwanda today.

In response to these attacks, several Hima warlords recruited Iru men into their armies to protect the southern part of Ankole which borders Rwanda. And, in some outlying areas of Ankole, people abandoned distinctions between Hima and Iru after generations of maintaining legal distinctions that had begun to lose their importance.

Another important player on the Ugandan political scene before and after independence was Busoga, the last of the four kingdoms we're going to look at and which was also identified as a princedom.

The kingdom traces its origin to the ascendancy of a clan that originated from Bunyoro in the 16th century. Members of the clan moved into the area of Busoga as part of Bunyoro's expansionist schemes and were led by Prince Mukama who is considered to be the founder of the princedom of Busoga.

Although called a kingdom, it was debatable whether or not Busoga was really a kingdom. It did not have central authority vested in a king or a queen as in neighbouring Buganda to the west, or as in Bunyoro where its rulers came from. It was, instead, ruled by several princes. The first rulers were the sons of Prince Mukama. And they really presided over a princedom, not a kingdom since none of them was a king.

The demographic profile of Busoga today reflects an impressive diversity. The kingdom is home to many people of different backgrounds.

The kingdom's history is also inextricably linked with that of Bunyoro and Buganda. People from both kingdoms had profound influence on the evolution of Busoga as rulers and administrators.

During the pre-colonial era, catastrophes such famines and epidemics forced many people to migrate to other parts of the Great Lakes region. It was these mass migrations which contributed to the establishment and growth of Busoga as a political entity. The people who migrated into the area of Busoga also brought with them their traditions and cultures from other lands.

When European explorers arrived in the area, they found that Busoga was well-populated and had plenty of food.

But a catastrophe in the form of sleeping sickness hit

22

the area in the first decade of the 20th century, forcing the evacuation of tens of thousands of people from the most densely populated parts of Busoga. More than 200,000 were forced to move in a period of 10 years and relocated to other parts of Busoga.

The southern part of Busoga constituted about one third of the kingdom's – or princedom's – land area and was the most populated. By 1910, it was empty.

The epidemic returned in 1940. It was not until 1956 that resettlement promoted by the government began again. But things were not going to be the same again and few Basoga returned to their traditional lands.

Other parts of Busoga affected by sleeping sickness, including the eastern areas and the northeast, were also depopulated.

The epidemic was accompanied by famine. And mass migrations made it very difficult and sometimes even impossible for people to work on the farms, making famine worse.

It was not until 1906 that Busoga had one ruler, a figurehead, who owed his power to the British colonial authorities. Before then, Busoga had semi-autonomous chiefdoms, at first under the influence of Bunyoro kingdom, and later of Buganda.

In fact, some of the chiefs in Busoga had been appointed by the kabaka of the Buganda kingdom. And it was believed that in some cases a number of them were descendants of Baganda chiefs who were given authority to rule over land in Busoga. They were not Basoga.

Others simply belonged to powerful landowning families in Busoga who had become self-appointed rulers over vast areas.

The British brought all these chiefs into an administrative structure called Lukiiko patterned after the Buganda traditional structures. They appointed a Muganda from Buganda, Semei Kakungulu, as the president of the Lukiiko and he became Busoga's first leader. But they refused to give him the title of "King" since they did not regard him as a real king.

The Basoga were not satisfied with this arrangement. And even among themselves, there were disputes between different chiefs and clans. And most of the people remained loyal to their chiefs and clans. Compounding the problem was the fact that the main traditional ruler, Semei Kakungulu – who wanted to be called a king – came from Buganda and not from Busoga and was not a Musoga.

As a result of all this, the Lukiiko collapsed, but not before the Basoga learnt a very important lesson. The Lukiiko structure had given them a taste of what influence they could have under the colonial administration if they had a king. It would elevate them to the level of Buganda and Bunyoro, kingdoms which had kings and which had more influence than any other traditional political entities in the Uganda Protectorate.

Still, Busoga has played a unique role in the history of Uganda as home to what once was the nation's second-largest city Jinja. Jinja is also the capital of Busoga and its commercial and economic hub.

Between 1920 and the 1970s, Jinja became a major industrial town, its growth fuelled by high cotton production and the completion of the Uganda Railway and the Owen Falls dam. It quickly became an agricultural and industrial centre with many factories and cottage industries including a well-developed infrastructure.

The town became a magnet attracting people from all parts of Busoga and beyond. Some of the most prominent new comers were Asian businessmen. And they played a major role in the development of Jinja, helping it to become one of the most vibrant commercial centres in the whole of East Africa. It also had the largest Asian population in Uganda.

And by independence in 1962, Jinja was home to 70 per cent of Uganda's industries. It was the nation's commercial centre.

Basoga itself as a whole continues to play a very important role in the development and national life of Uganda.

It's also strategically located along Lake Victoria and near the border with Kenya.

The area of Busoga – east of Buganda kingdom – is bordered on the north by the swampy Lake Kyoga which separates it from Lango territory; on the west by the Nile which separates it from Buganda; on the south by Lake Victoria which separates it from Tanzania and Kenya; and on the east by the Mpologoma River which separates it from various smaller ethnic groups such as the Badama also known as the Jopadhola, the Bugwere and the Bugisu – one of the most prominent in Uganda.

The princedom of Busoga also includes a number of islands in Lake Victoria, among them Buvuma, a chain of more than 50 islands, which is also the name of the largest island in this chain.

And together with Buganda, Bunyoro, Toro, and Ankole, it has given Uganda a unique identity as home to the most prominent kingdoms in East Africa.

All these traditional kingdoms no longer exist as single administrative units or as political entities. And they don't have the political autonomy they once enjoyed in varying degrees during colonial rule. But they continue to exist as cultural entities and play a very important role in the lives of the people who uphold tradition and are proud of their identities as members of traditional societies.

Before the advent of colonial rule, these societies existed as powerful independent nations. They had their own political and judicial systems. They were also conservative societies and resisted change including alien rule especially if it interfered with their traditional way of life and stripped traditional rulers of their power.

This included resistance to the modernising elite who spearheaded the struggle for independence and wanted to establish a modern state with central authority for the

25

entire nation of Uganda. As Colin Legum and John Drysdale state in *Africa Contemporary Record*:

"Uganda's basic political problems at independence in 1962 were dominated by the rigid and strongly-based determination of the kingdom of Buganda to maintain its distinctive identity – either by achieving a political ascendancy over the rest of the country as was largely the case in the heyday of Buganda's overlordship, or through secession.

Thus Buganda's politics had two parallel drives: the thrust to leadership for control of the modern political system, and thrust towards separatism.

Because Buganda lies at the heart of modern Uganda's economy and metropolitan development, and its people – the Baganda – were the best-educated and most sophisticated among the Ugandans, its threat to those who opposed it was formidable: more especially since the modern young Kabaka (Edward Frederick Mutesa) – a tough, shrewd and entirely inflexible leader – was strongly backed by the Buganda parliament, the Lukiiko, and supported by a closely-controlled system of rural government through a hierarchical chieftaincy system dependent on the Kabaka; these were buttressed by a closely-knit system of palace politics.

All these threads of Buganda's political power and authority were brought together in the Kabaka's hands on Mengo Hill – the seat of his palace and local parliament above Kampala.

Although Buganda offered the toughest problem to the modernising nationalists, it was by no means the only difficulty they had to face.

Each of the other three kingdoms – Toro, Ankole and Bunyoro – and the princedom of Busoga had their own well-structured political systems; each was suspicious of the modern political centre at Entebbe. Also they had traditional rivalries – especially between Buganda and

26

Bunyoro – this, however, had advantages for the nationalists since it helped prevent the southern kingdoms, mainly Bantu-speaking, developing an alliance of traditionalist interests.

Also, in the centre of the country, are two large areas, Teso and Lango, which – having entered into the modernising economic and education system at a fairly early age – constitute important political units; but they lack the strong tradition of centralised leadership.

To the North – among the Nilotic peoples stretching to the frontiers of the Sudan and the Congo – are scores of scattered ethnic groups who fared least well under colonialism, and who got into the modernising process several decades behind the Southerners.

Bringing them forward rapidly was an obvious priority for their own leaders; but those who undertook this task were in danger of being accused of wishing to favour 'the North' - with its Islamic contacts – against 'the South – with its Christian traditions and Bantu cultures. Both these elements were conveniently exploited by politicians in the North and the South.

Unlike most African countries, religion has played a role in Uganda's modern political development – mainly between Protestants and Catholics. Lately, too, the Muslim factor has been introduced.

In the politics of pre-independence the nationalist forces were divided and thus weakened; the traditionalists were strong but divided, and so less effective than they might otherwise have been. This enabled the running to be made by the Democratic Party, led by Mr. Benedicto Kiwanuka, which appealed nationally to the Catholic vote. His temporary majority in the Legislature was a challenge to both the nationalists and Buganda.

To defeat him Obote's Uganda People's Congress (UPC) entered into a political alliance of convenience with its arch political enemy, the Kabaka of Buganda." - (Colin Legum and John Drysdale, *Africa Contemporary Record:*

27

Annual Survey and Documents 1968 – 1969, London: Africa Research Limited, 1969, pp. 230 – 231).

Although the kingdoms still exist today, they are now part of a new political system and have been divided into administrative units introduced by the government of President Yoweri Museveni. And it's highly unlikely that they will regain their former power and glory.

Part Two:

The People

THE people of the area that came to be known as Uganda came from two directions: west and north.

Bantu ethnic groups migrated from west and central Africa about 2,000 years ago and settled in the southern part of the country. They were mostly farmers. They also had skills making iron including weapons and agricultural implements.

They also had their own ideas of social and political organisation and developed complex societies.

The earliest political structure which some of them established in the region was the empire of Kitara in the 14th and 15th centuries. It was followed by the kingdom of Bunyoro-Kitara and, centuries later, by Buganda and Ankole.

The other major wave of migration, which came from the north, was of the Nilotic people including the Luo and the Ateker. They entered the area from what is now Sudan around 120 A.D. They were cattle herders and subsistence farmers. And they settled mainly in the northern and eastern parts of the country.

Some of the Luo invaded Bunyoro and became an integral part of that kingdom.

Luo migration from the north continued until the 1700s and some of the new arrivals settled in eastern Uganda where they became integrated with the Bantu communities in that region. Others moved further east into what is now western Kenya and south into what is now northern Tanzania near Lake Victoria.

The Ateker – who are the Karamojong or Karimojong and the Teso – settled in the northeastern and eastern parts of the country. And some of them integrated with the Luo in the area north of Lake Kyoga.

The Teso or Iteso and Karamojong cluster of ethnic groups are the largest Nilotic populations in Uganda.

Arab and Swahili traders entered Uganda – before it became Uganda – from the east coast in the 1830s. They were followed by British explorers in the 1860s. The explorers were looking for the source of the Nile.

Protestant missionaries entered Uganda in 1877. They were followed by Catholic missionaries in 1879.

The United Kingdom acquired the area and placed it under the charter of the British East Africa Company in 1888. It became a protectorate in 1894 but not in its final form. Several other territories and chiefdoms were incorporated into the new colonial entity and it was not until 1914 that the Uganda Protectorate became fully established. It remained under British rule until independence in 1962.

The people of Uganda today are a diverse mix of ethnic, linguistic and cultural groups.

The vast majority are descended from the immigrants who came from the west and the north, waves of migration which formed a confluence in the Great Lakes region, one of the most distinctive parts of Africa.

None of the groups forms a majority of Uganda's population. And the 30 different languages spoken in the country represent an impressive array of ethnic groups and clusters.

In addition to Luganda, which is the indigenous language of the Buganda kingdom and most widely used local language, other main languages are Lusoga and Runyankore. Lusoga is the main language spoken in Busoga kingdom, and Runyankore or Lunyankole is the main language of Bunyankole.

Swahili is another important language in Uganda and other parts of East and Central Africa. One of its biggest advantages is that it transcends ethnicity and is not identified with any particular tribe or ethnic group, making it acceptable to people of different ethnic and cultural backgrounds.

But its status in Uganda is somewhat controversial. It was approved in 2005 as Uganda's second official language, after English, but it has not found wide acceptance across the country. The Bantu groups in the southern and southwestern parts of the country have not accepted Swahili as much as many people in the north – where it's an important lingua franca – have.

It's also widely used in the police and in the armed forces which had very many northerners – including Idi Amin – during the colonial period and in the first decade of independence.

The language was introduced by the Arabs and other coastal people and was promoted by the colonial authorities to facilitate communication. But it never became widespread in Uganda as it is in Tanzania and to a smaller degree in Kenya. However, efforts have been made by some Ugandan leaders to make it a national language. President Yoweri Museveni has done so, as did Amin.

In terms of demographic composition, three main

ethnic groups constitute most of the population in Uganda. These are Bantu, Nilotic, and central-Sudanic traditionally known as Nilo-Hamitic.

The Bantu are the largest. They include the Baganda, the largest ethnic group in Uganda, who live in the Central Province and who constitute 17% of the country's population; the Basoga who live in the southeast and make up 8.4% of the population; the Banyankole (9.5%) in the southwestern area; the Bakiga, (6.9%) in the most southwestern part of Uganda; the Banyoro (3%) in the mid-western area; the Batoro also known as Batooro (3%) who live in the mid-western part of the country; the Bagisu (4.6%) in the east; the Bahima (2%) in the southwestern area; the Bafumbira (6%) also in the southwest, and other much smaller ethnic groups.

The Lugbara who constitute 4.2% of the nation's total population live mainly in northwestern Uganda and the adjoining area of the Democratic Republic of Congo.

The north is mostly inhabited by the Nilotic who constitute the second-largest group after the Bantu. They include the Iteso who live in the northeast and make up 6.4% of the country's population; and the Langi in the central north who constitute 6.1%. President Milton Obote was a Langi.

The other major ethnic group in the north are the Acholi who make up 4.7% of the total population of Uganda.

The Acholi and the Langi speak almost identical languages. They're also the two largest ethnic groups in northern Uganda.

Traditionally, northerners have also provided the largest number of enlisted men in the Ugandan army since colonial times. Idi Amin, the most well-known, was a member of the Lugbara and the small Kakwa ethnic group which straddles the Ugandan-Sudanese-Congolese border in the northwest.

The most well-known Nilotic group in the northwest is

the Lugbara..

The Lugbara live in the highlands on an almost treeless plateau that forms the watershed between the Congo River and the Nile. The Madi live in the lowlands to the east. The two groups speak nearly identical languages and have strong cultural similarities.

Both groups raise millet, cassava, sorghum, legumes, and a variety of root crops. Chicken, goats, and, at higher elevations, cattle are also important. Maize, besides being grown for local consumption, is also used is grown for making beer. Tobacco is an important cash crop.

The Karamojong who make up 2% of Uganda's population live in the northeast. And the territory they occupy is considerably drier and largely pastoral.

Europeans, Asians and Arabs constitute 1% of Uganda's population. And there are other smaller groups who are equally an integral part of Uganda.

More than half of Uganda's population is under the age of 15. That's more than any other country in the world.

Non-indigenous people in Uganda include several hundred Western missionaries, a few diplomats and business people from many parts of the world.

Among all the indigenous groups in the country, probably the Baganda are the most studied. But they're not representative of Uganda in all fundamental respects in spite of the fact that their kingdom constituted the nucleus of the colonial entity when the British established the Uganda Protectorate more than 100 years ago.

And the ample literature about them, written during the colonial period and after independence, does not necessarily exceed that of other people in Uganda in all respects.

Yet they still constitute a microcosm of the Uganda nation. And much of what is written about them even today is applicable in other contexts including the study of other ethnic groups in the country because of the role they played in the evolution of Uganda as a political entity during colonial rule.

It was the largest of the former kingdoms in terms of area and constitutes slightly more than one-fourth of Uganda's total land mass.

Until 1967 when the kingdom was abolished, the Ganda society was highly centralised.

The *kabaka* ruled over a hierarchy of chiefs who collected taxes in the form of food and livestock. Portions were distributed through the hierarchy, eventually reaching the kabaka's palace in the form of tribute (taxes).

The kabaka made direct political appointment of all chiefs in order to maintain control over their loyalty to him. Many rituals surrounded the person of the king. Commoners had to lie face down on the ground in his presence.

There are more than 3 million Baganda today. And their kingdom comprises 52 clans, a social structure similar to that of other ethnic groups such as the Banyoro but not in all respects.

There may be some dispute on the number of clans but what is probably not indisputable is that there are at least 50 clans in Buganda. And at least six others claim clan status.

Within this group of 52 – or 50 – clans are four distinct sub-groups which reflect historical waves of migration to Buganda. They are Nansangwa, Kintu, and Kimera migration, and other clans, at least 20, which have either migrated to Buganda or have been created within the kingdom – mainly by the kabakas (kings).

The oldest group of clans is Nansangwa. It has six clans. And the name Nansangwa which is used to identify them collectively means "indigenous," a term similar to a word in the Nyakyusa language of southwestern Tanzania, *gwa kwanda* which means "the first" or "the first one"; plural form is *ba kwanda*. In Swahili or Kiswahili, it's *wa kwanza*.

One of the major clan groups traces its origin to

Bunyoro in the Kitara empire. The ancestor of these clans was Kintu, one of the most famous names in Bugandan – and Ugandan – history. He was the first ruler of Buganda and is considered to be its first kabaka, although some people contend that the institution of the kabaka was created later. Still, in terms of status, Kintu was the same as a kabaka (king).

The Kimera migration also traces its origin to the Kitara empire like the Kintu.

Kimera, the ancestor, migrated to Buganda with 11 clans. The Kimera migration was preceded by the Kintu migration which had 13 to 16 clans.

A group of related lineages constitutes a clan. And in terms of social organization, the Ganda society is patrilineal.

And traditionally, four or five generations of Baganda – with a common ancestry traced to one man and related through male forebears – constituted a patrilineage.

Clan leaders regularly summoned lineage heads who constituted a traditional council for the conduct of political and social affairs. And their decisions affected all lineages within the clan.

Many of these decisions regulated marriage which was always between two different lineages, forming important social and political alliances for the men of both lineages.

Lineage and clan leaders also helped maintain efficient land use practices. They also inspired pride in the group through ceremonies and remembrances of ancestors.

Most lineages maintained links to a home territory known as *butaka* within a larger clan territory. But lineage members did not necessarily live on that land.

Men from one lineage often formed the core of a village. Their wives, children, and -relatives-in-law joined the village. The people were also free to leave if they were not satisfied with local leadership. They took up residence with other relatives including in-laws and often did so.

Ganda villages, sometimes as large as 40 or 50 homes,

were generally located on hillsides, leaving hilltops and swampy lowlands uninhabited to be used for crops or pastures. The villages were established usually around the home of a chief or headman, providing a common meeting ground for members of the village.

The chief had many responsibilities. They included collecting tribute from his subjects and giving it to the king (kabaka) who ruled the entire kingdom of Buganda. The chief also distributed resources among his subjects and helped those in need. He also maintained social order and promoted solidarity among his people.

But the traditional structure came under severe strain through the years as social and political changes weakened and sometimes undermined its foundation. And the villages became more dispersed as the role of the chiefs diminished in response to political turmoil, population migration, and occasional popular revolts.

Many of the changes were a result of colonialism. The imperial rulers introduced a new system of government and institutions which undermined the traditional society in many ways, forcing the people to adopt new ways of life.

But the traditional of life was not completely destroyed by the colonial rulers and many people in Buganda today live the same way their ancestors did. Even many educated people who have been exposed to Western civilisation cherish their culture, values and traditions, solidly anchored in their collective identity as Baganda.

The family in Buganda is often described as a microcosm of the kingdom. The father is revered and obeyed as head of the family. His decisions are generally unquestioned.

A man's social status is determined by the nature of his company – the people with whom he associates – and by the patron/client relationships he establishes. And one of the best ways of establishing a patron/client relationship is through one's children.

Baganda children, some as young as three years old, are sent to live in the homes of their social superiors in order to cement ties of loyalty among parents and to provide avenues for social mobility for their children. Even in the 1980s, Baganda children were considered psychologically better prepared for adulthood if they had spent several years living away from their parents at a young age.

The Baganda recognize at a very young age that their superiors also live in a world in which they have to obey rules just like their subordinates do, although some of the rules may differ because of age differences.

Social rules require a man to share his wealth by offering hospitality. This rule applies more stringently to those of higher status. Superiors are also expected to behave with dignity, self-discipline and self-confidence. And adopting these mannerisms sometimes improves a man's opportunities for success.

Authoritarian control is also a very important part of culture among the Baganda. In precolonial times, obedience to the king was a matter of life and death. And few defied that.

Another very important aspect of culture among the Baganda is emphasis on individual achievement. The Ganda are taught that one's future is not entirely determined by one's status at birth or position in society. Individuals can succeed by working hard and by choosing friends, allies, and patrons carefully. The work ethic is very strong among the Baganda, complemented by good judgement.

In spite of the strong emphasis the Baganda place on ethnic solidarity and cultural pride as well as collective identity, they have not insulated themselves from external influence. And they have historically welcomed outsiders because their culture tolerates diversity.

Even before the coming of Europeans, many Ganda villages included residents from outside Buganda. Some had arrived in the region as slaves and were absorbed and integrated into the society. And since the early 1900s, many non-Baganda migrant workers stayed in Buganda to work on farms.

Also, marriage with non-Baganda was fairly common, and many Baganda marriages ended in divorce. After independence, Ugandan officials estimated that one-third to one-half of all adults marry more than once during their lives.

Traditionally, the economy of the Baganda relied on farming. And even today the majority of the people of Buganda depend on agriculture for their livelihood.

Unlike many other traditional societies in East Africa, cattle ownership played only a minor role in Buganda. And among those who owned cattle, many of them hired labourers from the north as herders.

The most important crop and food commodity was bananas. As a staple food, it sustained the population. It also fuelled population growth.

It also provided a solid foundation for the traditional economy. And it's still the most important food crop in Buganda even today and plays a major role in the kingdom's economy.

One of the biggest advantages of growing bananas is that the crop does not require shifting cultivation or bush fallowing to maintain soil fertility. That's one of the main reasons why Ganda villages existed as permanent settlements as they still do today.

In the Luganda language, bananas are called *matoke*. It's a term almost identical to *matoki* in the Nyakyusa language which I learnt when I lived for many years in Mpumbuli village in the area of Kyimbila in Rungwe District – traditional home of the Nyakyusa people – in the Southern Highlands of southwestern Tanzania.

This linguistic similarity is a common feature among Bantu languages showing they're related.

In Swahili or Kiswahili which is a product of Bantu

languages, the word for bananas is *ndizi*. But the term *matoke* or *matoki* is also used in colloquial Swahili. Many other Bantu languages have terms similar to that. And Luganda is one of the major Bantu languages in East Africa..

The Baganda have plenty of food. Besides bananas, they also eat cabbage, beans, peas, mushrooms, carrots, cassava, sweet potatoes, onions, various types of greens, eggs, fish, beans, groundnuts, beef, chicken, and goat meat among other foods. Fruits include pineapples, mangoes, passion fruit, and papaya.

Drinks include indigenous fermented beverages made from bananas (*mwenge*), pineapples (*munanansi*), and maize (*musoli*). A term close to *mwenge* in another Bantu language is *mbege*. Like *mwenge*, *mbege* is also an alcoholic drink made from bananas by the Chaga (or Chagga) of neighbouring Tanzania.

And the Luganda term *munanasi* is almost identical to *mananasi* which means pineapples in Kiswahili; *nanasi*, singular form. In the Nyakyusa language, it's *inanasi* in singular form and *mananasi* in plural form.

Coincidentally, both the Chaga and the Nyakyusa grow a lot of bananas just like the Baganda do.

The Baganda have very fertile land. Most of them are peasants who live in rural villages. Rich red clay on hillsides, a moderate temperature, and plentiful rainfall combine to provide a good environment for the year-round availability of bananas as well as the seasonal production of coffee, cotton, and tea as cash crops.

The Baganda are also well-known for their basketry, especially mat-making by women. The mats are colourful and intricately designed.

In Ganda society – or the Buganda kingdom – men traditionally cleared the fields and tilled the land while women planted crops. Men also engaged in commerce. There was a clear division of labour in many areas of life but those distinctions are now blurred in the modern economy.

However, differences remain in a number of areas. There are still many tasks which men or women are not supposed to do.

There are also many important economic activities which are no longer the exclusive domain of men. Some people, especially traditionalists, decry the change. Others, especially women and those of the younger generations, welcome it.

Some of the major changes which have taken place in the traditional society as a result of Westernisation include adoption of Christianity. It has transformed the traditional way of life so much that religious beliefs of the ancestors no longer play the kind of role they once did.

And the contrast is glaring. In the second half of the 1800s, most Baganda were practising an indigenous form of religion known as *Balubaale*.

It consisted of gods who had temples identified with them. The gods were each concerned with specific problems. For example, there was a god of fertility, a god of warfare, and a god of the lake.

The Baganda also believed in spiritual forces, particularly the action of witches, which were thought to cause illness and other misfortunes. People often wore amulets (charms) to ward off their evil powers.

The most significant spirits were the *muzimu* or ancestors who visited the living in dreams and sometimes warned of impending dangers.

But *Balubaale* is no longer practised by many people in Buganda. However, belief in the power of the departed ancestors and in witchcraft is still prevalent. And it probably will never die.

Another kingdom, Bunyoro, which played a major role in the establishment, evolution and growth of Buganda, had its own history of achievements which included the development of complex cultural and political institutions whose influence spread far beyond its borders.

Other political entities such as the princedom of Busoga, besides Buganda kingdom, also benefited from the achievements of Bunyoro. Their own institutions, at least some of them, were a byproduct of Bunyoro since some of these societies were partly established by the people who migrated from Bunyoro or were heavily influenced by Bunyoro.

The history of Bunyoro is a history of some of the greatest achievements – in terms of cultural, political, social and institutional development – in the history of pre-colonial Africa.

The kingdom was a product of the Kitara empire. It was originally known as Bunyoro-Kitara and was created when the empire of Kitara fell apart in the 16th century.

From the 16th to the 19th century, Bunyoro was not only the most powerful kingdom in a region that's now Uganda; it was also one of the most powerful in the entire East Africa. Even today, its traditional ruler, the Omukama, remains an important figure in Ugandan politics, especially among the Banyoro people of whom he is the titular head.

Traditionally, the Omukama was a divine monarch who also had the power to appoint local chiefs. And he held the kingdom together by invoking spiritual and temporal powers.

Located in western Uganda in the area east of Lake Albert, the kingdom of Bunyoro even today has strong traditional ties to Toro which was once part of Bunyoro. And the Bunyoro language is also spoken in Toro.

The Banyoro are Bantu. But their kingdom was founded by Nilotic people from the north.

Every Munyoro (singular) belongs to a clan which is a group of people who are descended from the same ancestor. They're therefore blood relatives.

The Banyoro are predominantly agricultural. But they also own cattle which play an important role in their lives. And while the kingdom's economy is heavily dependent

41

on agricultural commodities as is the case in most parts of Uganda, the discovery of oil in the kingdom is expected to transform this traditional society in significant ways.

The Banyoro also contend that they're entitled to a significant share of revenues earned from oil. According to a report in one of Uganda's leading newspapers *New Vision*, entitled "Why is Bunyoro Demanding A Share of Oil Money?":

"Bunyoro King Solomon Iguru and the late American literature professor Mason Cooley live thousands of miles apart but they have something in common. Cooley once said: 'Courage, determination and hard work are very nice, but not so nice as an oil well in the backyard.'

As though he were Cooley's student, Iguru is determined to reap from the oil in Bunyoro's backyard. So he has pulled out a four-page agreement his kingdom signed with the colonialists five decades ago and is demanding a share of the oil in the region.

1955 Bunyoro Agreement

The 1955 Bunyoro Agreement, signed between British Governor Sir Andrew Cohen and Omukama Tito Gafabusa Winyi IV on September 3, gives Bunyoro Kingdom rights to share in the region's wealth.

Section 36 of the agreement states: 'In the event of any mineral development, a substantial part of the mineral royalties and the revenue from mining leases shall be paid to the native government of Bunyoro-Kitara.'

Based on this clause, Iguru has petitioned the President to allocate his kingdom an oil exploration block and that when oil extraction begins, Bunyoro should receive a substantial percentage of the royalties.

Shem Byakagaba, a legal expert, argues that the agreement is binding because it has never been annulled. Oil being a mineral resource, he argues, it is covered under section 36 of the agreement.

The agreement was signed to reduce the impact of the military attack on Bunyoro by the colonial Government in the 1890s and the economic deprivation in the early 19th century. In 1934, the colonialists banned the Banyoro from exploiting the mineral resources. They lost control of salt mines and other minerals which, according to Iguru, deprived the kingdom of revenue. After negotiations, the agreement was signed, improving the relations between Bunyoro and the colonial government.

These rights were rescinded in 1966 when former President Milton Obote abolished kingdoms. With the restoration of cultural leaders in 1993, Iguru argues, Bunyoro is still entitled to mineral rights specified in the 1955 agreement.

The Kingdom's Stake

Iguru further argues that the National Oil and Gas Policy should indicate how cultural institutions will share the natural resources.

But the energy minister, Hilary Onek, says the policy and the Mineral Exploration Act allocate royalties to districts where the mineral resources are located; and a percentage is also paid to the land owners; who in this case is Bunyoro Kingdom.

Bunyoro Kingdom consists of Bulisa, Hoima, Kibaale and Masindi districts. Of these, oil has been discovered only in Hoima and Bulisa. If the royalty goes to districts and not the kingdom, only these two districts would benefit. For this reason, the Kitara Heritage Development Association argues that the kingdom should be treated as a region and not in terms of districts.

But the Cultural Restitution Act of 1993 which restored kingdoms only limits traditional leaders to cultural roles. It does not assign them the role of managing public resources. As a result, the traditional institutions like Bunyoro are not part of the administrative system.

Nevertheless, Byakagaba argues that the Cultural Restitution Act did not annul the Bunyoro Agreement of 1955. He calls for an amendment of the Act to allow kingdoms to manage mineral resources.

'And receiving such money would mean the kingdom will be exposed to the institutions of Auditor General to account for the funds received,' he adds.

But this also raises questions on whether Bunyoro has the institutions to ensure that funds are utilised efficiently for the benefit of the region.

What Needs to Be Done

If Bunyoro is to benefit from oil exploitation, the king should set up companies, which will be subject to government audits.

Onek says if Bunyoro has sufficient funds to invest in petroleum exploration, the Government will let them acquire an exploration block. He, however, cautions that allocating Bunyoro an exploration block is no guarantee that they will find oil. He adds that natural resources should be shared by the entire nation. He cautions against sectarian demands.

But Byakagaba argues, 'Bunyoro is not a tribe. It comprises various communities that include Baruuli, Bagungu, Bachope and the Banyoro.'

He adds that since Bunyoro will be most affected by oil exploration, they should take an proportionate share of the proceeds.

Banyoro's Other Demands

Already, the kingdom is seeking compensation from the Government for the Waraga oil site in Hoima, saying the area was an important spiritual centre. The kingdom says the government and the oil investors tampered with

44

the Bunyoro shrine, which was marked by mikooge (tamarind) trees. Waraga is said to be a spiritual centre set up by King Waraga, one of the oldest Bunyoro kings.

Bunyoro is also pushing for a university and petroleum institute at Kigumba, Masindi district.

Both the oil discovery and the 1955 agreement are not new. But campaigns for the 2011 presidential elections will start next year. Could the demand for royalties be a political calculation?" - (Raymond Baguma, "Why is Bunyoro Demanding A Share of Oil Money?," in *The New Vision*, Kampala, Uganda, Friday, 1 May 2009).

The demand for a significant share of oil revenues by the Bunyoro kingdom is also inextricably linked with the kingdom's demand for greater autonomy – now enjoyed by all the kingdoms but only in the cultural sphere – and assertion of its identity as a cultural and political entity in the context of Uganda.

It's a demand that has been shared by other kingdoms in Uganda through the years since independence and found its most forceful expression among the Baganda in the mid-sixties when they wanted to sccede and establish their own independent state.

The Banyoro may not have gone as far as the Baganda did in the mid-sixties, demanding full independence if their aspirations could not be realised in a federal context. But they have demanded nothing less in terms of autonomy. And they attribute many of the problems they face to the abolition of kingdoms by President Milton Obote in 1967. As Christopher Sabiti, chairman of a clans council of Bunyoro-Kitara, stated in his paper presented to a Federal Constitutional Seminar on the kingdom's status at Pope Paul Memorial Centre in Bunyoro, 9 – 10 May 1991:

"The immediate decline and decay of culture and cultural institutions in Bunyoro-Kitara in the last quarter of a century is largely and justifiably attributed to the abolition of kingdoms in Uganda.

The institution of the Omukama, as a cultural institution, is the one that embodies the cultural aspirations and accumulated wisdom of the people of Bunyoro-Kitara. Bunyoro-Kitara is part and parcel not only of Uganda but of the African continent where the role of culture in development, in the economy and in politics has been pronounced by many African leaders, politicians and intellectuals of no less stature than, for instance, Okot p'Bitek, Kwame Nkrumah, Sekou Toure, Modiba Keita, Chief Awolowo, Julius Nyerere, Tom Mboya, Jomo Kenyatta, Sedar Senghor and many others....

When we talk of 'nationality' we are talking for instance of Bunyoro-Kitara, Buganda, Busoga, Ankole, Acholi, Teso, Lango, etc., a common history, a common culture and which are capable, on their own, of self-determination....

We in Bunyoro-Kitara recognise the fact that the Banyoro have lost their cultural base. This is because the colonial masters pursued a policy of suppressing our people. By the time the NRM Government (of Yoweri Museveni) came to power this policy had not been reversed....

We have the right of survival and the right of self-determination. Every people should aspire to keep their cultural identity and to explore and exploit its positive potentialities....

We cannot run away from the fact that Uganda is a country of diverse cultures.

From north, from east, from south and from the west we have different languages, different cultures, different behaviour and different tendencies.

We should consider ourselves very lucky because what this means is that Uganda is culturally rich.

We are particularly fortunate because our different cultures tend to complement rather than conflict with one

46

another, even though some conflict would in fact be quite natural.

We, as Ugandans, must maintain this equilibrium on the basis of mutual respect, tolerance and understanding, knowing that our cultures are but different pillars of one nation. Those who find it impossible to respect this position are enemies of the people and have no place in this country.

One pillar of Uganda's cultural diversity is the Bunyoro-Kitara axis.

Few people can dispute the positive contribution of Bunyoro-Kitara to Uganda's history and cultural richness in so far as all conception of kingship in the interlacustrine region of East Africa originates from Bunyoro-Kitara; and in so far as the kingdoms in this region, especially Buganda which was more favoured by the climate, were found by the first European explorers like Speke and Grant to preside upon the most advanced civilisations in East and Central Africa.

If I am to disgrace a little, the alleged centrality of Buganda in Uganda is only geographical. As far as history and culture are concerned, however, it is Bunyoro-Kitara which is central to Uganda. This has to be recognised as such because it is historically true that what is Uganda today was not so long ago Bunyoro-Kitara. Nothing will change this fact. If therefore I was to propose a new name for Uganda, and I have no intention to do so, I would call her Bunyoro-Kitara.

Just when Bunyoro-Kitara was beginning to pick up culturally in the reign of the Omukama Sir Tito Gafabusa Winyi IV (1924 – 1967 years of reigning) Milton Obote struck, starting a fresh era of terror and violence upon our people; an era of such consequences that to-day even the name of Bunyoro-Kitara has been erased from the map of Uganda....

To parody Taban Lo Liyong, we have no Spencer to sing our jingles; We have no Shakespeare to dramatise our

47

tragedies, to extol our kings; We have no Milton to sing the music of our <u>mbadwa</u> gods – Kyomya Ruganda Amooti, Wamara Abooki, Ibona of Warage and many others; where is our Wole Soyinka, our Ecklas Kawalya, our Christopher Sebadduka to sing our clans, our Elly Wamala to give us a Kinyoro version of "Voila"?

Where is our Chaucer to tell of hidden humour in our underworld?

Where are they all?

Who is to praise our rustic beauties – do we have an Okot p'Bitek? Do we have a Thomas Hardy?

Where is our Endymion, our Lamia?

Cultural barrenness, I think, is a crime; and the responsibility for this crime lies with our oppressors.

In less than one generation, unless the present situation is reversed, the whole question of our culture will be a completely forgotten issue.

As a first step to redress the situation, the people of Bunyoro-Kitara have instituted a cultural revival forum known as Orukurato Orukuru Oruteraniza Enganda za Bunyoro-Kitara (a clans council of Bunyoro-Kitara) of which I have the honour to be Chairman, which is a forum of heads of clans, elders and their descendants.

As the name implies, we are trying to put our finger on the pulse of our society to promote unity through the clans, to revive culture through the clans and to create an institutional framework on top of existing cultural institutions.

We would like to improve the inner vitality and supremacy of our people and to cherish culture as an instrument of development and production. We wish also to refine our morals, behaviour and social responsibility. We want to preserve our heritage, both man-made and natural....

Bunyoro-Kitara is a geographical, cultural and historical entity with her own distinct cultural heritage and values.

The Banyoro are bound together by block and cultural bonds and form an entity with irresistible psycho-biological linkages.

Our cultural heritage, values and institutions, our customs and traditions, are enshrined in the unique institution of clans, which in turn have their focal point in the institution of the Head of Clans, that is to say the institution of Rukirabasaija Agutamba the Omukama of Bunyoro-Kitara.

The institution of clans in Bunyoro-Kitara and the institution of the Head of Clans in Bunyoro-Kitara are one and the same thing. That is the cultural nature of our society. One is not only a reflection of the other, but it is the other, truly.

The clans and the Omukama jointly symbolise continuity, unity, stability, perfection and excellence.

All the arts, sciences, etiquette and decorum, and the best in the whole range of human achievement depend on these institutions.

In the Omukama's palace all the clans range together to uphold what is best in Bunyoro-Kitara. There is no other place where this is possible.

The institution of the Omukama is the most central of all our cultural institutions, and to derogate from its honour and dignity is a direct insult upon our people.... The way to appreciate fully the institution of the Omukama is to become a Munyoro because this institution, as cattle is to a Munyankore or to a Karamojong, is integrated in the blood and outlook of our people.

Bunyoro-Kitara was an independent kingdom long before Uganda was known, and though oppressed, she was governed separately by the British through 1933 and 1955 Agreements. This status enabled Bunyoro-Kitara to preserve her customs, traditions and cultural institutions.

The 1962 Uganda Constitution confirmed this position by granting some form of Federal status to Bunyoro-Kitara in which the enjoyment of our culture was guaranteed. This position could not be altered without the express consent of the Banyoro.

Since the Banyoro were never consulted on the abolition of the 1962 Constitution nor consented to the abolition, it follows that the Orukurato Orukuru Oruteraniza Enganda za Bunyoro-Kitara would not like to be party to constitutional arrangements that do not in the first instance, guarantee the position accorded to Bunyoro-Kitara under the 1962 Constitution.

Ultimately, however, Bunyoro-Kitara demands full Federal Status in order to be fully autonomous in certain vital spheres. Similarly, we would not like to be party to a Uganda Constitution that does not guarantee the cultural diversity of the people of Uganda.

Lastly, but not least, it should be stated categorically that there can be no question of culture without land. You cannot have culture hanging in the air. The most important aspect of culture is, in fact, land. The sentiments of our people are very clear on this matter of land in Bunyoro-Kitara.

The land belongs to the Banyoro and their children and their children's children.

Whereas we warmly welcome other Ugandans to come and settle with us, and even marry our beautiful women, wholesale alienation of land to non-Banyoro in Bunyoro-Kitara must stop as it is going to cause a lot of problems in the future.

We cannot have a cultural base when the land is being taken away. The fact that our people are peace-loving and have so far been silent on the matter should not be mistaken for their consent.

I think in future the clans should be allowed to decide on who comes in and who goes out. The Banyoro themselves must control the land."

Christopher Sabiti, in his capacity as chairman of the

council of clans of Bunyoro-Kitara, articulates a position not very much different from what many people in other traditional kingdoms and societies in Uganda say.

And that is the imperative need for traditional entities to have autonomy in a number of areas in order to maintain their identities and pursue goals in their own political and social contexts to best serve their people.

It also goes to the heart of what constitutes Uganda as a single political entity. And it raises fundamental questions about the nature of relations between the country's various ethnic groups and even challenges the protocols of association the nation's different ethnic entities have with the central government in the context of a modern African state.

While Uganda remains a unitary state, to the consternation of many people who would like to see a federal structure instituted, the authorities at the centre realise that there is a need for decentralisation to enable the people to realise their aspirations across the spectrum at the local and regional levels. Decentralisation also defuses tensions between the central government and the regions, helping maintain peace and stability. It also strengthens national unity and neutralises secessionist tendencies.

One of the areas in which the regions have demanded autonomy – as well as help from the national government – is education. Bunyoro is a typical example. As Milton Wabyona, a government minister for youth and cabinet secretary in the kingdom of Bunyoro Kitara, stated in his article, "Bunyoro Needs A Full University, Not Just an Institute," in Uganda's *Monitor* newspaper, 29 April 2009:

"One of the good things that the government has done through the decentralisation policy is to bring education closer to the people. Uganda today has several regional public universities or at least a major tertiary institution in every region.

51

Bunyoro, however, still remains a peculiar case where even the former National Teachers' College in Masindi is no more. I started hearing of a university in Bunyoro way back in 1998 and the signpost of Bunyoro University at Kwebiha Hostels in Hoima has since been standing although it has steadily faded – no indication of even a university book store.

Three years ago, government agreed to give Bunyoro a government-aided public university (like Gulu, Busitema, Mbarara etc), and one of the major faculties would be that of Petroleum Engineering. This was a very well-intended strategy given the oil and gas exploitation in the Albertine Valley which would provide the nearest stations for practical lessons.

The proposal to locate the university at the current Kigumba Cooperative College in Masindi District was highly welcomed since there was already some basic infrastructure that would enable a quick start.

Surprisingly though, the existence of Bunyoro University remains a dream to date. We hear it has now been decided that an Institute of Petroleum Engineering is going to be established as a constituent College of Makerere University, and relocate the present Cooperative College to Tororo.

Is an Institute of Petroleum Engineering in Bunyoro equivalent to a university?

Can the reasons the Banyoro sought a university all be summarised in this institute or the intentions and mission be well accomplished by just the institute?

Is transferring Kigumba Cooperative College to Tororo the price for having an Institute of Petroleum Engineering in Bunyoro?

Bunyoro Kitara region is rated among the regions with the lowest literacy levels in Uganda. This is also one of the poorest regions where over 70 per cent of the population can hardly afford quality education, and tertiary education in urban Uganda.

The medical superintendent of Hoima Referral Hospital recently told me that the major challenges that had caused the biggest numbers of deaths at the Hospital were lack of blood and medical staff.

The doctor lamented that Hoima Referral Hospital was the only one in Uganda that did not have a Nursing School or any Paramedical Institute and a Blood Bank.

These are some of the reasons why Bunyoro needs a university. When President Museveni visited Karuziika Royal Palace last year, he publicly instructed the Ministry of Education to operationalise Bunyoro University as a public government-aided university starting with the 2009/2010 academic year. I am not sure if this position has since changed or it has just not been followed up.

What is hindering the accessibility of such basic services to our region; is there anything we should be doing differently to get our share of the national cake?"

Others also demand their share of the national cake. They include the kingdoms of Toro and Ankole and the princedom of Busoga which together with Bunyoro and Buganda have earned Uganda distinction as the most "aristocratic" nation in East Africa.

But the Banyoro feel that they have a special claim to the wealth generated by oil found in their territory. And it has potential for disaster.

If the oil wealth is not distributed well, Uganda could have a situation similar to what has happened in the Niger Delta in Nigeria where the indigenous people have not benefited from the sale of oil pumped from under their feet.

Since the early 1950s when oil was discovered in Nigeria, the country has earned more than $600 billion. Yet the people of Nigeria are still some of the poorest in the world, and the indigenes in the Niger Delta some of the most exploited. They have nothing to show for all that wealth earned from their soil except polluted land and water including fish, endangering the lives of millions of people in the region.

There's no guarantee Uganda will avoid all that even if the situation does not become as extreme as it is in Nigeria. And the expectations of the people of Bunyoro are as high as those of their brethren in the Niger Delta. They bank on oil. According to *The East African*, Nairobi, Kenya, in its report, "Bunyoro Hopes of Oil Wealth Rise as Colonial Treaty is Found":

"The Bunyoro region's hopes of getting a lion's share of the oil wealth from recent discoveries in the region now hinge on a 54-year-old colonial era agreement that assigned the kingdom "a substantial share" of proceeds from any mineral wealth exploited on its territory.

Kingdom officials tell *The East African* that they have initiated high-level contacts with the central government to bargain for a fair share of oil wealth based on an agreement signed between Bunyoro and colonial authorities in 1955.

Article 36 of the agreement between Bunyoro Kitara Kingdom and the British Protectorate government states: 'In the event of any mineral development taking place, a substantial part of the mineral royalties and revenue from mining leases shall be paid to the native government of Bunyoro Kitara.'

The agreement document, a copy of which *The East African* has seen, has surfaced soon after the executive approved a new National Oil and Gas Policy that designates the oil resource as a national asset.

Energy-sector sources say the government is still in the process of designing a new oil revenue law that will determine how oil proceeds are shared out between the central government, local authorities and landowners.

Bunyoro argues that while kingdoms were abolished in 1966 by the first Milton Obote regime, its agreement with the protectorate government was never annulled, so still remains valid and should therefore be the basis for any negotiations over royalties to the region.

Officials from the kingdom told *The East African* that they have written to President Yoweri Museveni on the matter, and are eager to start negotiations.

Bunyoro Kitara, one of the most powerful kingdoms in 19th century East Africa, is located in western Uganda, home to the oil-rich Albertine Rift.

The kingdom still commands respect among a significant portion of the country's citizenry, and is currently involved in litigation with both the Ugandan and British governments, which if successful could strengthen their claim for a lion's share of the oil wealth.

However, Hilary Onek, Minister for Energy and Mineral Development, said that the matter has not yet reached his desk, but advised that the government follow the new policy of managing oil wealth as a national asset.

'We now have a policy we are following, so if Bunyoro feels aggrieved, they should instruct their Members of Parliament to try to change the law through the House,' said Mr Onek.

On the part of the kingdom, what should be negotiated with government is not the validity of the agreement, but the share it deserves, an important issue not stated in the colonial pact.

'We originally wanted a share of 5 per cent, but we have since reviewed our position, and we would like to negotiate the share with government because the agreement does not state it,' said Yadezi Kiiza, newly installed Prime Minister of Bunyoro.

Hundreds of thousands of barrels' worth of oil reserves have been confirmed in ongoing exploration activities in Uganda, validating prospects of substantial revenue from the country's next main export.

As far as oil wealth sharing is concerned, the National Oil and Gas Policy stipulates that the biggest share will remain in national coffers, while smaller shares go to the local government in the exploitation area and the landowner under whose property the oil is drilled.

This amendment was a response to the kingdom's demands for inclusion in revenue sharing, since the policy at the time focused on things like capacity building, licensing and monitoring exploration, and obtaining geological and geophysical data that would help attract oil companies to invest here.

'Nobody will be denied royalties, because according to the policy, royalties shall be paid to government, local government and the landowner, who (in the case of a kingdom) should be the king holding the land of the kingdom in trust,' said Mr Onek.

However, the kingdom of Bunyoro, unlike other traditional establishments in Uganda, does not hold land, which means that the new policy technically excludes it from the list of direct beneficiaries

It is also known that drilling and production of oil has been strategically situated in game reserves in Bunyoro, which are owned by the state.

Where the oil wells are not in game reserves, like a number in Bulisa County, the land is communally owned. It appears that local governments in Bunyoro region could ultimately be the prime beneficiaries there.

'But we are not ready to be knocked off the list so easily; we shall claim our share,' said Bunyoro Premier Kiiza.

With the colonial-era agreement in hand, Bunyoro has received a boost to ts campaign to reclaim its land.

Apparently, the British colonialists gave away parts of Bunyoro to the neighbouring Buganda and Toro kingdoms in 1899 in retribution for the resistance to colonial dominance by the then king of Bunyoro, Kabalega Cwa II.

Bunyoro has filed a case in the Uganda courts, and is to file another in Britain, both in pursuit of its land.

It is clear that Bunyoro fears losing out in the wake of the government's repeated assertions that natural resources are national assets, and the areas containing them can only gain a little extra in provision of health services.

Mr Onek said, 'Some parts of the country do not have minerals, but they should benefit from national mineral assets. However, the government, through the policy, recognises the areas where the minerals are mined, and for that reason gives them something extra.'"

But in many countries, newly-found wealth – in whatever form – is not always what's portrayed to be. In all the African countries where oil has been found, it has been both a curse and a blessing.

In fact, in most cases oil wealth has been more of a curse than a blessing. And Uganda is no exception. Bunyoro may become the Niger Delta of the Great Lakes region, if not of the entire East Africa.

Even neighbouring Tanzania with its substantial mineral wealth hardly gets anything from its newly-found wealth. Most of it goes to foreigners who work in collusion with many government officials to exploit the people.

Right next to Bunyoro, in the south, is the kingdom of Toro which once was an integral part of the large empire of Kitara. The empire included areas of present day central, western, and southern Uganda; northern Tanzania, western Kenya, and eastern Congo. The Bachwezi are credited with the founding of the Kitara empire.

In addition to founding the empire of Kitara, the Bachwezi are further credited with the introduction of the unique, long-horned Ankole cattle, coffee growing, iron smelting, and the first semblance of organised and centralised government, under the king.

No one knows what happened to the Bachwezi. There is a popular belief among scholars that they simply got assimilated into the indegenous populace and are, today, the tribal groups like the Bahima of Ankole and the Batutsi of Rwanda.

Usually, the Bahima and the Batutsi are tall and have a light complexion. It's said that the Bachwezi also looked that way. They're also herders of the long-horned Ankole cattle just as the Bachwezi were. And the blood of the Bachwezi still runs through the veins of many people in the kindoms of southwestern Uganda including Toro.

The Toro kingdom enjoyed peace and prosperity for more than 100 years after it was founded by a prince who was the son of the king of Bunyoro. He broke away from his father and declared himself king of the southern province of Bunyoro. And he was warmly received by the people of Toro province – the Batoro or Batooro – who became his subjects.

Like other Africans in most traditional societies, the Toro are conservative in general but probably more conservative than many other people in Uganda. For example, old taboos which have been observed for centuries are still observed today even when they're counterproductive. Some have to do with certain kinds of foods. Many Toros still don't eat those foods to their detriment.

Modernisation – a term synonymous with Westernisation – has had an impact on Toro society, sometimes in a profound way, but not enough to change the traditional way of life in all its aspects. The Toro themselves can best describe their society and how they live:

"The people of Toro are known as the Batooro (singular, *mutooro*; adjective, *kitooro*; language, *rutooro*). They are a proud tribe of about one million strong.

They enjoy a rich culture of oral tradition, tribal customs, indigenous handicrafts, patriotism, and very high self-esteem.

Like all African children, batooro children are taught to respect and value their elders. They are also taught to love and be proud of their tribe and country.

Pride in being a mutooro is a value of paramount importance that is inculcated into every mutooro child from birth. There are certain behaviors, manners of speech and personal conduct, therefore, that are considered to be beneath a self respecting mutooro.

Traditionally, for instance, a mutooro is not supposed to speak words or make any utterances that distort the mouth and make the person look undignified. Unfortunately, the observance of this norm made it difficult for many batooro to pronounce certain foreign language words effectively! A mutooro has to make a conscious effort to break with tradition in order to utter some foreign expressions that end in an open mouth or a distorted facial expression.

A mutooro must be dignified at all times. In fact the tribal name, batooro, is rooted in the word "omutooro" which means "ceremony".

Literally translated, batooro means "the ceremonious ones"; a possible reminder of the practice of putting on one's best attire to welcome guests, as carried out and passed on to us by our ancestors. This ideal of dignity has, at times, collided with modern lifestyles.

Traditionally, it is undignified to walk very fast, and yet we must do it in order to keep up with today's pace of life and work requirements.

A mutooro must sit down to have a meal, and must proceed to eat slowly, taking one's time to enjoy the meal. A mutooro must not eat on the run!

This is another clash with modern life where fast food is the order of the day.

Traditional eating habits of the batooro left them prone to malnutrition as their choice of acceptable cuisine was very limited. Many of the good, nutritious foods that abounded in their kingdom were taboo.

A mutooro did not eat "birds" or their eggs. So, for the longest time, the batooro did not eat chicken or eggs. A mutooro did not eat "frogs" (a derogatory name generalized over everything from the water, including fish).

It was ironic, therefore, that while Toro boasted of having two fresh water lakes teeming with delicious tilapia nilotica, they considered it beneath them to eat the fish!

A mutooro did not eat the meat of any animal that had upper teeth, because such an animal was like a dog. This ruled out pork.

For some reason, batooro women were, and still are, expected to be even more dignified than their male counterparts. Whatever the taboo was, it went double for the women.

As modern times slowly caught up with us, we slowly started breaking some of our long held traditions. To this day, however, there are some old batooro women who will not allow chicken, fish or pork to be cooked in their kitchens!

Social makeup

The batooro society has traditionally been demarcated along "economic activity" lines, rather than caste.

Two classes could be identified, the bahima and the bairu. The bahima were the cattle keepers, the bairu the land tillers.

The two classes lived symbiotically as one provided the needed milk, meat and butter; and the other provided the needed food products. Today, the line of demarcation is growing very faint.

Since the old days, the batooro have always considered themselves as one people, under the unifying leadership of the Omukama (king) who was, until 1967, their ruler. Under the Uganda constitution, the kings are recognised (only)as cultural heads of their tribe.

Family Ties and Genealogy

Every mutooro child born is automatically a member of the batooro tribe.

Apart from the standard naming ceremonies, which take place at a very early age, there are no strict rites of passage, as found in some of the other Uganda tribes.

The system of naming batooro children is rather unique, and needs some explanation for the sake of our Western friends.

Every mutooro child has his or her own "last name"! The reason for this is very simple. Kitooro names must have a meaning; they must say something about the prevailing conditions or circumstances surrounding the birth of the child being named.

A name may reflect a significant event that was taking place at the time of the child's birth.

There are standard names for twins and the children following those twins.

The names are chosen by the family elders who sit around a good meal, sipping some local brew, and informally choose a name for the new baby. This takes place when the baby is four days old in the case of males, and at three days old, in the case of females.

With the coming of Islam and Christianity, in the late 19th century, the tradition of giving the child a religious name on top of the traditional name started.

While the tribal name is always in the tribal language, the religious name may be an Arabic name for Muslims, an English or French name for Christians. Bible names are very popular with Christians.

Since circumstances and events are ever-changing and not the same for every child, it would be erroneous to give an umbrella "family" name to all the children born into a family.

Our Western friends may ask, 'How does one know one's blood relations?' The answer is simple; through one's clan.

The clan system is what lays out our lineage and establishes our blood relationships. This is very important and is taken very seriously to avoid inbreeding.

It is taboo for a mutooro to marry someone from his/her clan or that of his/her mother's clan. This taboo applies even to distant cousins several times removed.

An exception to this taboo has traditionally been granted to our royal family, who, in an effort to maintain their true blue blood lines, have been known to break with tradition and marry within their own or their mother's clans.

Every mutooro child born takes his/her father's clan. When 'girl meets boy,' they must disclose their clans and those of their mothers at the very outset, to avoid violating a taboo.

Empaako (names of endearment)

Unique to the people of Toro, Bunyoro (and one or two tribes in Tanzania and Congo) is a special name of endearment, respect, praise, etc., known as empaako.

In addition to the name the world will know the child by, each mutooro child is given one of the ten 'empaako' names.

The empaako names are: *Abbala, Abbooki, Abwooli, Acaali, Adyeeri, Akiiki, Amooti, Apuuli, Araali, Ateenyi, Atwooki.*

There is a twelfth one, *Okaali*, reserved only for the Omukama (king). *Okaali* is very special in that it is not for everyday use to greet the Omukama. It is used on occasions when our tradition elevates the Omukama to the rank of our gods.

When we 'worship' our king, we address him as *Okaali*. The Omukama is the only mutooro with two *empaako* names. Upon becoming the Omukama, no matter what his *empaako* was before, he takes the *empaako* **Amooti**. This is the one we use to greet him on an everyday basis. On special, traditional ceremonies and rituals, we greet him as *Okaali*.

Contrary to the norm that kitooro names have a kitooro meaning and say something, the empaako names do not mean anything in rutooro; because they really are not kitooro names in origin. They were brought to Bunyoro by the Luo who invaded Bunyoro from the north.

They have been assimilated into the language and tagged with special meanings; for instance, Akiiki bears the tag *'Rukiikura mahaanga'* (savior of nations); Abwooli is the cat; Ateenyi is the legendary serpent of River Muziizi, etc. The empaako is used for respect, praise and love.

Children never call their parents by their real name; they use the empaako. Calling one's parents by their 'real' names is considered a sign of disrespect, even poor upbringing.

When batooro greet each other, they use the empaako, e.g. *'Oraire ota, Amooti?'* (Good morning, Amooti?). Amooti is the empaako in this example. Very often one will hear an exchange like this:

> *'Empaako yawe?'* 'What's your empaako?'
> *'Adyeeri, kandi eyaawe?'* 'Adyeeri, and what's yours?'

Having established each other's *empaako*, they proceed to exchange greetings.

Our relatives, close friends, and (sometimes) important members of the community, expect us to know their *empaako*. It is impolite not to know it!

Sometimes one tries to ask other people while the relative, friend, important person, etc. is not hearing, so one can greet them without having to ask them their *empaako*.

Grownups can generically apply the *empaako* **Apuuli** to young male children whose *empaako* they do not know. The *empaako* **Abwooli** may be equally applied to young female children." - ("The People of Toro," from "Toro Kingdom").

The Toro are also known for their traditional dances. They have two main ones. One is called *ntogoroo* and the other one is known as *amatimbo*.

The dances are accompanied by drum beating and metallic sounds. Both male and female dancers wear metallic beads woven together on soft material around their legs, producing sound when the people dance.

Their traditional foods are millet, sorghum, sweet potatoes, bananas, peas, beans, groundnuts, green vegetables including cabbage, and firinda.

Milk and butter are also part of their diet. The cattle-owing Bahima provide milk and butter, while the agriculturalist Bairu grow food crops.

In spite of the abundance of fish in the lakes of Toro, fish has never been an integral part of the Toro diet because of cultural taboos as explained earlier.

The Toro kingdom is, at this writing in 2009, led by a child-king; Prince Oyo Nyimba Kabamba Iguru Rukidi IV, the youngest monarchial ruler in world history.

He ascended the throne in 2004 when he was three-and-a-half years old following the death of his father, King Kaboyo Rukidi III. This marked the beginning of a challenging and exciting period for the people of Toro. The child-king was listed in the *Guinness Book of World Records* as the world's youngest reigning monarch.

Regents were appointed to assist the newly enthroned young king as his gurdians to initiate him into his role as the cultural leader of the Toro kingdom.

King Oyo's regents included Ugandan President Yoweri Kaguta Museveni; the king's paternal uncle Prince James Mugenyi; his paternal aunt and godmother Princess

Elizabeth Bagaaya, and the other kings in Uganda.

King Oyo's palace is one of the most beautiful and most recent permanent structures in Fort Portal, the capital of Toro. It was renovated and a new giant circular administrative tower building was built with donations from Libya's President Muammar Qaddafi.

The coronation of the child-king was one of the most important events in the history of post-colonial Uganda especially with regard to the revival of the kingdoms allowed by President Museveni but only in the cultural context without any political power being wielded by the traditional kings as was the case before, mainly during the pre-colonial era.

President Museveni has said that the decision taken by the National Resistance Movement (NRM) government to re-instate kingdoms and support cultural institutions was deliberate in order to maintain and preserve the cultural roots of Uganda's traditional societies.

But it was also a strategic move. The decision was clearly political. It was intended to win support across the spectrum and help consolidate his power.

The ascension to the throne by the child-king of Bunyoro was one of the most important political developments in the new politics of the New Resistance Movement government of President Museveni which re-instituted the old kingdoms.

It was also of highly symbolic significance in terms of relations between traditional rulers and the national government. Museveni himself played a major role in the king's coronation as one of the regents. His coronation was also a major achievement for the Toro.

But in spite of his status as king, he was still a child. As *The New York Times* stated in its report from Uganda on 7 October 2004 entitled "For His Royal Playfulness, Goats, Sheep, but Nary a Toy":

"There are some distinct advantages, Oyo Nyimba

65

Kabambaiguru Rukidi IV acknowledges, to being a king.

'You have many people who like you a lot,' said King Oyo, as he is known to his one-million-plus subjects in western Uganda's Toro Kingdom.

'Like' is actually an understatement. At ceremonies in his main palace in Fort Portal, worshipers get down on their hands and knees in front of him, kiss at his feet and bring him valuable offerings like live goats and sheep.

Then there is the overseas travel that comes with wearing a crown.

Uganda is a poor country, so destitute in fact that the average citizen makes not enough in an entire year to afford a plane ticket to see the world. But kings ride business class. King Oyo has been throughout Africa and has made trips to Europe and America as well, meeting a variety of V.I.P.'s in the process.

All the same, as King Oyo sat on a leopard skin that had been draped over an armchair in his other palace, in Kampala, the other day, he said that being king has some drawbacks for someone of his generation.

'My life is very different from most 12-year-olds,' said King Oyo, fidgeting with a rubber band tied around his royal wrist and looking both kinglike and kidlike at once.

Sure, King Oyo plays video games, goes off to school every day – where his classmates and teachers just call him Oyo – and runs around the palace yard with his three dogs when he is not doing homework.

But King Oyo also has bodyguards and rules over an elaborate administrative structure that includes a prime minister, a board of regents and a variety of parish councils. He cannot just walk out his front gate and mingle with the other children in his upscale neighborhood. Sometimes, he says, he feels a bit trapped.

'Sometimes I wonder, 'Why am I a king?' he said. That question is easy to answer, at least as far as the rules of the kingdom go.

His father, King David Patrick Olimi Kaboyo II, died

when Oyo was 3½. In the Toro Kingdom, women cannot rule so Oyo's mother was out, as was his older sister. Although rather young, Oyo was crowned nonetheless on Sept. 11, 1995, earning a place in the *Guinness Book of World Records* as a toddler king.

Africa has a smattering of kings, in Ghana, South Africa and, most notably, Swaziland, where his majesty has drawn criticism for his free-spending ways and for his practice of plucking a virgin girl out of the masses during an annual festival to become one of his many queens.

King Oyo is dull in comparison. He does not even have a girlfriend. His mother controls the household spending. There has not been any particularly dramatic palace intrigue under his nine-year reign.

Uganda's kingdoms go back hundreds of years but former President Milton Obote outlawed them in 1967 as part of his effort to consolidate rule.

It was not until 1995 that the government of President Yoweri Museveni reinstated the country's four kingdoms – Buganda, Ankole, Bunyoro and Toro – although more as cultural institutions than the ruling monarchies they once were.

King Oyo's father was living in exile when the kingdoms were reinstated. He returned to much rejoicing among the Toro. His rule was short, however.

Soon, young Oyo was wearing the Toro crown, which has a giant white feather sticking out the top, and the gold-laced vestments.

He had no choice, really. It was his duty to become the 12th king of Toro.

That is what the queen mother, Best Kemigisa, regularly reminds him. 'Bringing up a king is a serious responsibility,' she said of her role in the kingdom.

Despite her best efforts, sometimes King Oyo's lack of enthusiasm for the role is rather hard not to see.

Some observers said his face seemed glum last month at the anniversary of his coronation, which along with his birthday is celebrated with much pomp among the Toro.

Weeks before the big day there is a cleaning of everything in the palace. When the anniversary arrives, his subjects gather and King Oyo is presented with the royal ax, the royal bow and arrows and the royal sword. The royal troupe plays drums and royal flutes.

There is a milking of the royal cows, which is performed, as one might expect, by royal milkmen. At one point, King Oyo must stride around the grounds, although palace functionaries scurry ahead of him to ensure that his feet touch straw mats and not the earth.

The royal publicist is on hand, reminding the uninitiated that it is an 'abomination' to turn one's back to the king. Most are too busy gawking at King Oyo to consider such a thing.

There was a recent attempt to further curtail the limited powers of Uganda's kings, but the country's many monarchists would have none of that.

Mr. Museveni, the president who some critics say acts like a king, proposed that Parliament be allowed to remove kings who violate the Constitution.

An uproar ensued and the government has since backed away from the proposal.

King Oyo's mother – who sits by his side, adjusts his crown and helps him navigate the difficult world of being a king – voiced her kingdom's disapproval with the government plan. 'These members of Parliament are below the king,' she said bluntly. 'They are subjects of the king. How could they remove him?'

As she spoke, King Oyo, who had earlier excused himself, was outside the palace kicking around a soccer ball, acting more kid than king."

The child-king has helped to put his kingdom in the international spotlight partly, if not mainly, because of his age.

But the kingdom of Toro also has a number of tourist

attractions. They include the king's palace, the Amabere ga Nyina Mwiru caves, the Nyakasura hills, crater lakes such as Saka, Kigere and Nyabikere, and Kibale Forest National Park.

It's a small kingdom in terms of area. But with a population of more than one million and a rich and dynamic history, the Toro kingdom stands out as one of the most prominent traditional societies in Uganda and in the entire East Africa.

Another major kingdom is Ankole, one of the big four in the Great Lakes area of what later came to be known as Uganda.

While the identity of Toro is inextricably linked with that of Bunyoro, the former being a product of the latter, that of Ankole stands on its own in a number of ways. But Ankole was also heavily influenced by Bunyoro, as were the rest of the kingdoms, since Bunyoro was the most powerful in the Great Lakes region for centuries.

The people of Ankole are called Banyankole or Banyankore; in singular form it's Munyankole or Munyankore. And the Ankole kingdom is also known as Nkore.

It was traditionally ruled by a monarch known as *mugabe* or Omugabe of Ankole, a title equivalent to that of the *kabaka* in the Buganda kingdom.

The establishment of the Ankole kingdom is attributed to the Hima, also known known as Bahima, who conquered the Iru (Bairu) before the 19th century. They became a dominant force in the Great Lakes region until they were replaced by the colonial rulers as the dominant power.

The Banyakole are also well-known for their cows known as Ankole. In fact, one of the most famous breeds of cows in East Africa is Ankole. Ankole cows are known for their long horns.

But there are also fears that it may be a dying breed. They have been an integral part of life in the Great Lakes region for centuries. But that may no longer be the case after a few decades. According to a report from Uganda published in *The New York Times* and entitled "Herd Extinct: The Ankole Cow Could Disappear Within 50 years," 27 January 2008:

"Gershom Mugira comes from a long line of cattle-keepers. His people, the Bahima, are thought to have migrated into the hilly grasslands of western Uganda more than a thousand years ago, alongside a hardy breed of longhorns known as the Ankole.

For centuries, man and beast subsisted there in a tight symbiotic embrace.

Mugira's nomadic ancestors wandered in search of fresh pasture for their cattle, which in turn provided them with milk.

It is only within the last few generations that most Bahima have accepted the concept of private property. Mugira's family lives on a 500-acre ranch, and one sunny day in November, the wiry 26-year-old showed me around, explaining, with some sadness but more pragmatism, why the Ankole breed that sustained his forebears for so many generations is now being driven to extinction.

As we walked down the sloped valley path that led to a watering hole, we found a few cows lolling beneath a flat-topped acacia. They looked like the kind of cattle you might encounter in Wisconsin: plump and hornless creatures with dappled black-and-white coats.

Mugira, a high-school graduate, was wearing a pair of fashionably baggy jeans and spiffy white sneakers. To a modern African like himself, he said, the most desirable cattle were the American type: the Holsteins.

In recent decades, global trade, sophisticated marketing, artificial insemination and the demands of agricultural economics have transformed the Holstein into the world's predominant dairy breed.

Indigenous animals like East Africa's sinewy Ankole, the product of centuries of selection for traits adapted to harsh conditions, are struggling to compete with foreign imports bred for maximal production. This worries some scientists.

The world's food supply is increasingly dependent on a small and narrowing list of highly engineered breeds: the Holstein, the Large White pig and the Rhode Island Red and Leghorn chickens. There's a risk that future diseases could ravage these homogeneous animal populations.

Poor countries, which possess much of the world's vanishing biodiversity, may also be discarding breeds that possess undiscovered genetic advantages. But farmers like Mugira say they can't afford to wait for science. And so, on the African savanna, a competition for survival is underway.

Mugira was just about to tell me what made the Holsteins so valuable when suddenly, Dr. Grace Asiimwe, a veterinarian and my guide through western Uganda's ranchlands, shouted, 'The Ankoles are coming!'

In the distance, I glimpsed a bobbing line of white horns swooping down the hillside. Without a word, Mugira dashed down the dirt path, hopped over a fallen tree branch and disappeared around the side of a huge weed-covered anthill.

'He has to keep them separated,' Asiimwe told me, lest the Ankoles gore the Holsteins.

We found Mugira by the watering hole, whistling and waving a wooden switch called an *enkoni*, frantically trying to keep his Ankoles away. His herdsmen were supposed to bring the two contingents to the water at different times, but someone made a mistake.

'You know, in Uganda, we have to look for survival of the fittest,' Mugira said once he finished sorting out the confusion.

'These ones, they are the fittest,' he went on to say, gesturing toward his Holsteins.

71

In physical terms, there was really no contest between the tough Ankoles and the fussy foreign cattle, which were always hungry and often sick. But the foreigners possessed arguably the single most important adaptive trait for livestock: they made money. Holsteins are lactating behemoths. In an African setting, a good one can produce 20 or 30 times as much milk as an Ankole.

Mugira explained that, unlike most of his peers, he was holding onto some longhorns, mostly for sentimental reasons. His father, who died in 2003, loved his Ankoles. One of them wandered over and nuzzled Mugira, who placed his hand gently on its forehead.

In the days before Christianity arrived in this part of Africa, the Bahima made offerings of milk to herdsman gods. Their language contains a vast catalog of cattle names, which refer to characteristics like color and hide pattern. This cow was called Kiroko, indicating it had some white patches on its face.

The ideal Ankole, Mugira told me, has a lustrous brown coat and gleaming horns that curve out and then inward, forming a shape like a lyre. 'They are naturally good,' Mugira said. 'They are beautiful. In our culture we preferred these. But then we developed another culture, from Western culture.'

The Food and Agriculture Organization (FAO), an agency of the United Nations (UN), recently reported that at least 20 percent of the world's estimated 7,600 livestock breeds are in danger of extinction.

Experts are warning of a potential 'meltdown' in global genetic diversity. Yet the plight of the Ankole illustrates the difficulty of balancing the conflicting goals of animal conservation and human prosperity.

An estimated 70 percent of the world's rural poor, some 630 million people, derive a substantial percentage of their income from livestock. Increase the productivity of these animals, development specialists say, and you improve dire living standards. The World Bank recently published a report saying it was time to place farming 'afresh at the center of the development agenda.' Highly productive livestock breeds, the World Bank asserts, are playing an important role in alleviating poverty.

'You do have local animals with various kinds of disease resistance and whatever other kinds of things you don't want to do away with," said Chris Delgado, an agriculture policy adviser at the World Bank. "But there's a problem: They are kept by very poor people, and they don't want to stay poor.'

Every cow in the world is the product of some human agency. The extinct feral ancestor of all cattle, the auroch, was a fearsome horned creature that could grow to be six feet tall.

There are two theories about the taming of wild aurochs. The traditional view holds that it happened around 6000 B.C. in the Fertile Crescent. But recent archaeological and genetic evidence suggests that domestication may have first occurred in Africa 2,000 years earlier, in the then-lush plains of the eastern Sahara. Then, beginning around 2,000 years ago, Arab merchants introduced humped cattle of Indian origin to East Africa, which were crossed with the indigenous longhorns to produce breeds like the Ankole.

For millennia, changing a breed's genetics through husbandry required a long trial-and-error process. But today it can happen in an evolutionary eye blink. Multinational breeding companies, many of them based in the United States, collect semen from prime bulls, freeze it and export it to the developing world.

Official estimates say there are about three million Ankole cattle in Uganda and smaller populations in bordering nations. An unknown – though by all accounts large – percentage of them are in the process of being turned into something else.

After one cross with a Holstein, the brown Ankole cow will produce a black calf with darkened horns. After two, the horns will shrink and a dappled coat will appear. The third generation will basically look like American dairy cattle. With each cross, the offspring will produce more milk.

The World Bank estimates that 1.8 million small-scale farmers in East Africa are benefiting from such genetic changes to their cattle and that some 100 million cows and pigs are created through artificial insemination in poor countries each year. Those numbers substantially understate the extent of genetic interchange, because half the offspring produced by artificial insemination are male and spread their genes the old-fashioned way.

To see the evolution in Ugandan dairy cattle, I visited a farmer named Jackson Sezibwa, who lives down a reddish dirt path outside the central Ugandan town of Mukono. A weather-beaten man of 46, Sezibwa greeted me in a torn, muddy shirt. He showed me to the metal-roofed stall where he keeps his Holstein, Kevina.

Before he received the cow, Sezibwa said, he was hungry and destitute. All he owned were some banana trees and a one-room house roofed with thatch. Then he and his wife were given Kevina by a charity called Heifer International. Founded in 1944 by Dan West, an Indiana farmer, Heifer's mission is to take quality livestock to impoverished places. In Uganda, the cattle breed Heifer prefers is the Holstein. 'The American cow,' said Dr. Margaret Makuru, Heifer's deputy country director, 'once you feed it, it is a factory.'

Like any factory owner, Jackson Sezibwa had to think about inputs and outputs. Making milk requires energy, which means eating grass. Holsteins require much more grass than Ankole cattle, but unlike Ankoles, which need to roam, Holsteins can be kept in pens.

Sezibwa owned just a small plot of land, so the Holstein was perfect for him. All day long, Sezibwa refilled Kevina's trough with feed, a mixture of elephant grass and protein-rich leaves and legumes that he grew in

74

his field. Each time he milked the cow, he fed her a store-bought meal full of nutrients. Otherwise, his largest expense was medicine.

Holsteins originated in Northern Europe and were taken to America in the 19th century. They don't have any resistance to tropical diseases like trypanosomiasis – colloquially known as sleeping sickness – and East Coast Fever, which is spread by ticks.

With intense maintenance, Sezibwa's cow functioned marvelously. Kevina churned out around six and a half gallons of milk a day. (A typical Ankole would have given him between a quarter and a half gallon.) His family drank some of the milk, and he sold the rest, netting around $100 a month after expenses.

In a country where an estimated 85 percent of the population lives on less than $1 a day, that's substantial income. The money finances school for Sezibwa's six children. There were ancillary benefits too.

Kevina was impregnated four times via artificial insemination. Sezibwa gave away her first calf to a neighbor, in keeping with Heifer's philosophy of 'passing the gift.' The next two – both males – he sold to farmers eager to acquire Holstein genetics, making enough profit to build himself a nice brick house. He kept the fourth calf, another female, for the future. Heifer also paid to install an underground system that harnessed methane from the cows' manure to power gas burners and a light inside his house.

Jackson Sezibwa is just one man, but Uganda's economy is made up of millions like him. Agriculture accounts for 30 percent of the country's gross domestic product, and 10 percent of that comes from the livestock sector.

The World Bank's October report claimed that 'G.D.P. growth originating in agriculture is at least twice as effective in reducing poverty' as other types of growth. The report pointed out that the industrialization of Europe and North America that began in the late 18th century was preceded by a period of farming innovation, and that the Green Revolution that took place between the 1940s and 1960s catalyzed Asia's fantastic economic growth.

During the Green Revolution, scientists invented high-yielding strains of corn, wheat and rice and planted them around the Third World, and they also promoted the introduction of better livestock.

But then, broadly speaking, foreign-aid donors moved away from such interventions, which were viewed as meddling with the free market, and shifted financing priorities to areas like education and AIDS. Today, even after recent increases, the World Bank devotes less than 10 percent of its development assistance to agriculture, down from 30 percent a quarter-century ago.

Recently, the notion of helping poor farmers by making farming more lucrative has been dusted off by a new generation of economists. And Bill Gates and the Rockefeller Foundation have promised to finance a second Green Revolution. But governmental aid agencies have been slower to rediscover the importance of agriculture. Farming initiatives now account for just 4 percent of the assistance distributed by the Organization for Economic Cooperation and Development (OECD), a group of the world's most developed nations.

The U.S. Agency for International Development (AID) budgeted $392 million for agricultural programs last year, including a significant proportion to promote milk production. Crossbreeding is an important component of its strategy.

In Uganda, where the agency recently completed a five-year, $8 million dairy-modernization project, about half the money went toward artificial insemination. One partner in the program was Land O'Lakes International Development, the aid arm of the Minnesota butter company. 'We should be able to do farming as a business, not sentimentally,' said Dr. Paul Kimbugwe, the Land

O'Lakes country manager. 'Making money means you have to crossbreed. And crossbreeding means that you are doing away with the genetics of that cow,' meaning the Ankole, "which I also encourage.'

Not everyone in Uganda, however, agrees that the foreign breeds are an upgrade.

President Yoweri Museveni once imposed a ban on imported semen. Museveni belongs to the Bahima ethnic group. When he was a baby, in a sort of Bahima baptism ritual, his parents placed him on the back of an Ankole cow with a mock bow and arrow, as if to commit him symbolically to the defense of the family's herd. Museveni, now in his 60s, still owns the descendants of that very cow, and he retains a strong bond to the Ankole breed.

Two years ago, I accompanied a group of Ugandan journalists on a day-long trip to one of the president's private ranches, where he proudly showed us his 4,000-strong herd of Ankole cattle. At one point, a reporter asked if the ranch had any Holsteins. 'No, those are pollution,' Museveni replied. 'These,' he said, referring to his Ankoles, 'the genetic material is superior.'

If the Ankole cattle are able to mount a comeback, it will be because circumstances have endowed them with a unique set of defenses, both evolutionary and political. Members of President Museveni's ethnic group populate the upper ranks of Uganda's government.

Some prominent Bahima have started an organization devoted to preserving Ankoles, under the patronage of a one-eyed army general who spends his free time painting rapturous portraits of cows.

One afternoon, at a pricey restaurant in Kampala, I had lunch with the organization's chairman, Samuel Mugasi. Dressed in a dapper gray suit and a French-cuffed pale blue shirt, he told me he was a civil servant and part-time rancher.

'They have tasted the money,' Mugasi said of the

farmers who switched to Holsteins. 'They are excited about having these big earnings, and they are forgetting the cultural aspect.'

Kimbugwe, the Land O'Lakes representative, has a ready reply to such arguments. 'Culture – fine, it's good to have,' he said. 'But first, the stomachs.'

He views the Ankole as an atavistic indulgence for the country's elite.

Once, cattle were like currency, and the wealthy displayed their status by maintaining huge free-ranging herds.

Competition for land is forcing cows onto smaller pastures. Uganda has one of the highest birth rates in the world, and despite its poverty and diseases like AIDS, the population has more than doubled since 1980.

There's a long history of tension between the Bahima and an agriculturalist ethnic group, the Bairu, which coexist in western Uganda, at times less than happily. This is a common dynamic across Africa.

In Rwanda, a similar ethnic conflict between cattle-keeping Tutsis and farming Hutus culminated in genocide in 1994.

A number of experts say the 'ethnic' war in Darfur is really a fight over grass.

Uganda has not experienced that level of conflict, but the local newspapers are filled with stories of violent skirmishes between farmers and encroaching pastoralists. This is one reason that some say Holsteins represent the future.

Rwanda, now ruled by longhorn-loving Tutsis but trying to address the causes of the genocide, is enthusiastically encouraging the breed's introduction, with assistance from the U.S. Agency for International Development (USAID).

One of the biggest dairy farmers in western Uganda, Kezekia Rwabuhenda, told me he was the first person in his area to adopt Holsteins, back in the 1970s. At the time, he said, many traditionalists maligned him, saying he was conspiring to 'slaughter' the cattle they loved. 'Afterwards, when they realized what the cross was producing, they started visiting me, asking for a bull,' he said through a translator.

The elderly rancher still kept a hundred Ankoles, but they were for his wife, who was attached to them. He was sure that when he died, his children would dispatch them all to the butcher shop.

No one knows how many Ankole cattle exist. 'We've been saying the Ankoles are 50 percent of the national herd, but I don't think that's true anymore,' said Dr. Denis Mpairwe, an animal scientist at Uganda's Makerere University. 'The crossbreeding the last five years has been so intense.'

The International Livestock Research Institute predicts that if present trends continue, the Ankoles could go extinct within 50 years. But Mpairwe says he believes it could happen much sooner.

I went with Mpairwe to visit Uganda's cattle country earlier this fall, along with Dr. Okeyo Mwai, a Kenyan biotechnology specialist who works for the livestock institute.

I lived in Uganda between 2002 and 2004, and I couldn't believe the change.

Hillsides where graceful brown Ankoles once grazed by the hundreds were now dotted black and white. 'Look at the calves,' Mwai said, as our pickup truck passed a herd. 'Almost 100 percent are crosses.' He pointed up toward the hilltops, normally gently rounded and green, but now sandy in large patches from overgrazing.

The two scientists are studying how high-producing cattle interact with the African ecosystem. If cows are like factories, you could say an Ankole is powered by a water wheel, while the Holstein requires a nuclear reactor.

The principle of the 'tragedy of the commons,' perhaps the most famous metaphor in ecology, is a cattle parable. It was first described by a 19th-century British economist and popularized by the biologist Garrett Hardin in a 1968 *Science* magazine essay about human overpopulation.

Hardin was trying to refute the view that an unregulated free market invariably produces beneficial outcomes.

'Picture a pasture open to all,' Hardin wrote. The benefit of adding a single calf went to each individual farmer, while the cost of adding that calf (the grass it would consume) would be distributed to all pasture users. 'Each man is locked into a system that compels him to increase his herd without limit — in a world that is limited,' he wrote. The commons, he predicted, would inevitably be picked clean.

With the introduction of the Holsteins, something similar seems to be happening in Uganda. Farmers aren't literally increasing the sizes of their herds, but they are creating herds that consume unsustainable amounts of dwindling resources. And something else is being obliterated: genes.

Each time a farmer crossbreeds his Ankoles, a little of the country's stockpile of adaptive traits disappears. It isn't easy to measure genetic 'dilution.' What is evident, however, is that the Ankoles possess much worth saving. For instance, their horns, often seen as ornaments, actually disperse excess body heat.

Holsteins don't like heat. While a poorly adapted animal can survive for years in a harsh ecosystem, even a slight worsening of their conditions can have devastating effects.

One rancher I met, John Kamiisi, told me that he'd lost his herd of Holsteins in a 1999 drought. He only avoided ruin because he kept some Ankoles, which could live on less water.

Kamiisi told me he loved his sturdy Ankole bull 'like my own life' but said he was starting to crossbreed again for financial reasons.

Another elderly rancher said his whole Holstein herd died during Idi Amin's dictatorship, when chaos and inflation made it difficult to buy the imported medicines the cattle needed. He started again with a few Ankoles his neighbors gave him out of pity.

'For countries on the equator, I think in almost all cases the Holstein is very poorly suited – maybe the least-suited breed,' says Dr. Les Hansen, a professor at the University of Minnesota and a leading expert in cattle genetics.

Often farmers are making decisions that are informed not by science, he said, but by sales pitches devised by multinational breeding concerns. 'As I travel the world,' Hansen adds, 'my biggest challenge is countering all of the misleading marketing propaganda.'

The world market in cattle breeding is controlled by a handful of companies, several of them based in the United States. The companies maintain facilities where they extract semen from bulls, keep genetic databases, publish rankings and cultivate a sort of bovine star system.

Two legendary Holsteins, Chief, born in California in 1962, and Elevation, born in Virginia in 1965, fathered tens of thousands of offspring in their lifetimes – and beyond, since their sperm was cryogenically frozen for future use.

Hansen's research suggests that every Holstein is descended from Chief and Elevation, and that 30 percent of all the Holstein genes in the world are traceable to those two bulls.

That has created a serious problem with inbreeding, which has adverse effects on fertility and mortality.

But overseas markets like Africa are, so to speak, virgin territory. According to industry figures, American companies exported 10 million "doses" of cattle semen in 2006. In Uganda, a company called World-Wide Sires, the international marketing arm of two American breeding cooperatives, is working with aid agencies to increase dairy production.

'The proof is in the bucket,' said George Nuwagira, a dairy farmer who is also the World-Wide Sires sales representative for western Uganda.

I met him one morning in the market town of Kabwohe. A stout, garrulous fellow, he was wearing a yellow baseball cap with a smiling cartoon cow on it. He ushered me into his insemination center, a narrow tumbledown storefront that also sold sodas.

At one end stood a wooden counter that was decorated with a flier advertising a bull named Earl, 'the Dairyman's Dream,' which pictured Earl's daughters posed in such a way as to accentuate their enormous milk-swollen udders. Behind the counter sat a metal tank filled with liquid nitrogen.

Nuwagira unscrewed its cap, and a thick cloud of white vapor billowed out. He retrieved a cluster of brightly colored plastic straws filled with premium semen.

We were at the far end of the global semen supply chain.

Nuwagira handed me an empty green straw. It was marked with the name 'Theseus' and a long serial number, which indicated that the semen it had contained was collected at a facility near Plain City, Ohio, on Dec. 30, 2004. Three weeks before, he used Theseus' semen to impregnate one of his own Holsteins.

Nuwagira took me to see the expectant mother. On the bumpy ride to his farmland in a breathtaking green valley, he told me that he was from the west's agriculturalist ethnic group, not the Bahima. He didn't care about the Ankole. 'To me as a modern farmer, the horns don't mean anything,' Nuwagira said.

He didn't name his cows like the Bahima but instead referred to them by numbers. He told me he owned just 35. 'You know, it was used as a status symbol in the past, to have so many head of cattle,' he said. 'Those who had hundreds wouldn't sit with those who had less than 30. But these days, things have changed. When you talk of animals they don't ask you the numbers. They ask you the production.'

Nuwagira's biggest problem was getting his product to market. 'You feed them, they will give you the volumes, but there are times when we find we are stuck having nowhere to sell it,' he explained.

Milk is perishable, and Uganda is a country where roads are bad and refrigeration is rare. The dairy trade in rural areas is largely controlled by bicycle vendors who sell raw milk from aluminum jugs.

There used to be a more sophisticated network of government-affiliated dairy cooperatives, but most of these were dismantled in the 1990s, during a World Bank push for market liberalization. The private sector was supposed to fill the gap but never did. Anyway, some Ugandan tribes don't drink milk. They're lactose-intolerant.

Crossbreeding follows the logic of the arms race. All the ranchers I met complained that Holsteins required expensive upkeep, and many didn't want to abandon tradition. But they've had to change because their neighbors are changing.

The volume of milk produced in Uganda doubled between 1993 and 2003, but in the absence of a surge in demand or improved delivery systems, the product has literally flooded the market. As the price per liter has fallen, dairy farmers have had to rearm with Holsteins just to maintain their usual profit margins.

International organizations realize that increased productivity means little if it's not accompanied by market growth. That's why the U.S. Agency for International Development is spending millions across Africa to promote dairy cooperatives and pay for advertisements inspired by America's famous 'Got Milk?' campaign.

But changing distribution and diets isn't as easy as changing breeds. 'A lot of consumers don't understand how important milk is,' says Jim Yazman, a livestock

83

specialist with the agency.

Economic forces can push a breed to extinction with frightening swiftness.

In Vietnam, where pigs are the most important livestock species and the government has encouraged leaner foreign breeds, the percentage of indigenous sows has fallen to 28 percent from 72 percent since 1994, and 13 of the 15 local breeds are classified as either extinct or in danger.

There were several million Red Maasai sheep in Kenya until the 1970s. Then, in just 15 years, indiscriminate crossbreeding with woollier imported sheep nearly drove them out of existence. But the wool sheep fared poorly in the Kenyan environment, in part because of intestinal parasites to which the Red Maasai were resistant. By the time that was discovered, though, purebred Red Maasai were almost impossible to find.

Many tropical breeds may possess unique adaptive traits. The problem is, we don't know what is being lost.

Earlier this year, the U.N.'s Food and Agriculture Organization released its first-ever global assessment of biodiversity in livestock. While data on many breeds are scant, the report found that over the last six years, an average of one breed a month has gone extinct. 'The threat is imminent,' says Danielle Nierenberg, senior researcher at the Worldwatch Institute, an environmental group. 'Just getting milk and meat into people's mouths is not the answer.'

As the world's climate warms, and the environment becomes more inhospitable to the major breeds, humanity might need the genes that allow animals like the Ankoles to flourish in the African heat. The challenge is to safeguard the resource.

There are two possible approaches: putting the animals in cold storage, or changing the economic equation.

Proponents of the first option desire something like the Svalbard Global Seed Vault, a doomsday depository for plant species that an international consortium is building in the Arctic Circle.

But storing sperm and embryos is far more expensive and technically difficult.

Biodiversity advocates say that it would be preferable, anyway, for breeds like the Ankole to go on living in their pastures. The most obvious way to do that would be to create incentives to entice farmers to keep them.

But even those who want to save endangered breeds recognize that subsidizing unproductive livestock in hungry countries is problematic.

In November, at a conference sponsored by the International Livestock Research Institute in Nairobi, Kenya, Dr. Edward Rege, the organization's biotechnology director, gave a speech listing several 'inconvenient facts' about conventional wisdom in the field, adding that conservation approaches can effectively amount to 'saying that farmers should remain poor.'

The best hope for the Ankoles may reside at a modest, terraced complex on a breezy hillside in Uganda overlooking Lake Victoria in the old colonial town of Entebbe.

It was constructed by the British in 1960, at the height of the Green Revolution, as an artificial-insemination center and a staging ground for introducing new breeds – animals that mostly died off during the subsequent wars and dictatorships.

Now called the National Animal Genetic Resources Center and Databank, the facility's new mission is to save indigenous animals like the Ankoles by giving them better care and selectively breeding them to compete in production.

The center keeps a dozen bulls of different breeds, including two immense Ankoles that once belonged to President Museveni.

Twice a week, technicians collect semen, which is used to inseminate cows at government farms or else packaged and sold directly to farmers.

If it's successful, the program could offer a model to other developing nations. If, on the other hand, the Ankole cattle can't be saved even with such government support, it's difficult to imagine how any threatened breed will survive.

'They can produce milk and they put on meat,' said Dr. Dan Semambo, the center's executive director. 'People don't know what they have.'

Ugandans rave about the fresh milk out west, and every rancher I visited there served me a cup. It has a delicious sweet thickness.

No matter how well nourished they are, though, the Ankoles probably can't produce as much milk as the Holsteins.

Instead, the breed's salvation could lie in the slaughterhouse.

President Museveni says he believes that Ankoles make exceptional beef cattle and wants to export their meat. Some studies suggest that Ankole beef is unusually lean and low in cholesterol. Mpairwe and his colleagues at Makerere University are completing a study in which Ankoles and crossbreeds were kept on nutrient-rich diets. In early December, the cattle were slaughtered and an 'expert panel' of faculty and students conducted a taste test, with encouraging results.

Shortly before I left Uganda, I convened an expert panel of my own. We met one evening at Le Petit Bistro, a European-owned restaurant that serves Kampala's best steak.

While we waited for our orders, I went back to the kitchen to meet the cook, Everest Neretse, who was wearing a white chef's jacket and flip-flops. He told me he came from the west. 'Ankole cattle, they are the best,' he said. 'I can tell in the tenderness.'

I had my filet with a little garlic butter. When I cut into it, rich reddish juices spilled out, and the texture was so soft that I hardly needed to chew. It was almost as if you could taste the contentment of an unbounded life on the open range.

The panel agreed: it was extraordinary, it was beautiful and in no time every trace of the Ankole was gone."

But even when the Ankole cow is no more, if the breed will indeed be gone one day, the people in the Great Lakes region who have relied on this domesticated animal for centuries will continue to live the same way.

They're still going to have cows, only of a different breed or breeds.

And the people of the Ankole kingdom, well-known as cow owners and as farmers, will always be among those who will benefit the most from the new breed or breeds of cows as they continue to live their traditional way of life but only with different results.

The cows they're going to have are going to be more productive, giving them more milk, hence more economic security and better health.

But it will also be tragic. The old ways, of owning the Ankole cows and all that it entails in a cultural context including its spiritual dimension since this breed of cows has been an integral of life in the Great Lakes region for centuries, will be lost forever.

Just like other Africans, the Ankole are a proud people. They're proud of their culture and traditional way of life. And they don't want to lose it. They're also proud of their ethnic identity as Ankole different from other ethnic groups.

And theirs is "the land where milk and honey freely flow down the village paths."

But they also have differences among themselves. One of those differences has to do with the status of the Ankole kingdom – whether or not it should be restored. As one Ugandan observer states about the Banyankole and their land:

"Ankole is a blend of mystery and fascination. Cattle are part and parcel of a Munyankole from Ankole. The Ankole land is a mixture of various vegetation animals, birds as it is a mixture of personalities.

Life in this place is a comical contrast of extremes. On one hand you have long-horned cattle that seem to have more horn and bone than flesh. Probably weighed down by the grotesquely oversize horns, they crawl along, passive and pondering.

In contrast, the people are full of life and passion and basically bursting with good health. They move about briskly and gaily, calling out greetings to one another with an enthusiasm that rubs onto the observer.

When you crack a joke to a Munyankole, chances are he will laugh loud and long and then tell you a much better version of the same joke.

But when you talk about Omugabe the mood slows down. Either, 'We have no king and never you say that around here!' Or: 'Museveni and Co. have denied us our right to a Kingdom and enjoyment of culture.'

The bitter division about their kingdom – or what is left of it – is obvious.

One fine afternoon in September 1967, Ankole's Enganzi (Prime Minister) left his Mbarara office to grab a bite at home. He intended to return that afternoon to complete the kingdom's duties for the day.

A casual phone call shattered his programme: 'Don't you bother – or dare – return to office. Kingdoms have been abolished.'

The kingdom's offices were taken over by the government. As the Baganda broke down and wept, there was jubilation in many parts of Ankole.

The 1971 incoming of Idi Amin raised hope for restoration of kingdoms, especially when he returned the body of the late king of Buganda, Sir Edward Mutesa II.

A delegation of Baganda met Idi Amin, asking him to

restore the Buganda Kingdom.

But 'Big Daddy' casually told them to forget the idea. He did not like the idea of an embrace when he thought a handshake was enough.

The Banyankole apparently got the message fine. When a delegation of elders – led by former Omugabe Sir Charles Gasyonga – met Big Daddy later that year, they presented a signed memorandum asking him not to restore the Ankole monarchy.

Amin pumped their hands happily in a fresh round of greetings. He soon gave Gasyonga's heir-apparent Prince John Barigye an ambassadorial job.

(Prince) Kahigiriza denies this story. But it is supported by articles from the press of the day and the testimony of witnesses.

Ankole today is split in two

On one hand, is a self-assured Banyankore Cultural Foundation (BCF) saying to hell with Omugabe. The monarchy, argues the anti-Omugabe camp, encouraged class distinction based on occupation and is the embodiment of division in Ankole. It was a caste system – people were ranked in hierarchy: the King on top, then the Bahinda royal clan, Bahima pastoralists then the Bairu cultivators.

So reviving it means reviving social discrimination and injustice because the institution belongs to the Bahinda as a clan and was supported mainly by the Bahima.

'With the abolition of the monarchy, the basis for social differences was removed because the Omugabe was a basis for social differences,' says Makerere law don Dr Jean Barya.

'The unity that has been growing in Ankole would be in danger if the monarchy were restored because these social categories and differences were slowly dying out, especially with education, access to economic resources and political power by the majority of Banyankole since 1967.'

BCF draw their strength from the fact that popular opinion in Ankole does not favour the monarchy. And equally importantly, from the fact that President Museveni is openly against the idea of Omugabe. Knowing they are politically correct seems to boost their confidence.

On the other hand is a much less assured Nkore Cultural Trust (NCT) parading an inferiority complex in articulating their demands. They are openly timid because of the lack of enough public and political sympathy.

'We do not want to be seen against government,' says James Kahigiriza. 'But the kingdom has not been restored because of funny politics. Those who object do so because of jealousy and sectarian tendencies, that is why they are playing the Bairu-Bahima card.'

In 1993 the National Resistance Council (NRC) enacted the Traditional Institutions Statute that stipulated that any community could revive the institution of traditional leadership if the people of the relevant community so wish.

But it did not say how that (whether people want) should be determined.

Article 246 (2) of the Constitution says 'In any community, where the issue of traditional or cultural leader has not been resolved, the issue shall be resolved by the community concerned using a method prescribed by Parliament.'

This, says, Barya, was put there specifically for Ankole and means that since there is a dispute the matter has never been resolved.

'The NRC as a whole was opposed to general restoration of kingdoms – not those from Buganda,' says Barya.

'What Museveni did (at that time thinking of Buganda which was demanding) was to hold a closed session of the NRC in April 1993 in which he persuaded – or cajoled –

them to allow the Buganda monarchy to be restored.

'Buganda had threatened to vote against the Movement in the CA (Constituent Assembly). But the CA could not make a law addressing Buganda alone; so they made a general one – Traditional Leaders (Restitution of Properties) Statute 1993.

'The only kingdom automatically returned by law is that of Buganda. The others would only be returned through consultation and negotiation, because government was not sure whether people in those areas wanted the kingdoms restored.'

Barya adds that Museveni's only concern is that since the institution is unpopular it could cost him votes. But he does not wish to antagonise the monarchists so he gives them hope that the Omugabe will be restored through discussion and compromise.

'That way he gets votes from both sides – each side in the hope that it will triumph. Otherwise the matter would have been resolved one way or another, by now, says Barya.

The kingdom regalia is also in dispute. NCT says it is Barigyc's property. But BCF says it is a symbol of kingship but belongs to the kingdom rather than an individual. And that when the kingdom was abolished in 1967, the regalia reverted to central government – like all the others.

Subsequent developments since the enacting of the Traditional Institutions Statute have not favoured the pro-Omugabe camp." - ("Monarchies: Ankole Kingdom").

Yet the people of Ankole are united as a single cultural entity whose ethnic bonds transcend political differences. Traditionalists and modernists, even ethnic chauvinists and nationalists who want one Uganda as a single nation, are all inextricably linked, constituting one of the most well-known ethnic groups in Uganda and in the whole of East Africa.

Like other Ugandans, they are a people with their own traditional homeland, their own customs and way of life handed down through the generations. And they cherish the memory of their history and keep alive the traditions of their ancestors just as other Ugandans do.

Although Uganda is a product of a few old kingdoms and many smaller independent chieftaincies, its traditional landscape – in terms of prominence and importance – is dominated by only a few traditional institutions.

The communities which have been organised in traditional institutions of kingdoms – and princedoms – are the Baganda under the *kabaka*, the Banyoro under the *omukama*, the Banyankole under the *omugabe*, the Batoro also under the *omukama* like the Banyoro, the Basoga under the k*yabazinga*, the Alur under the *rwoth-obima*, the Ateso under the e*morimori*, and the Bakonjo under the *omumbere*.

The kingdom of Ankole reached a level of sophistication during pre-colonial times which even impressed European explorers. They were amazed at the sophisticated and cultured societies they found not only in Ankole but in neighbouring kingdoms.

The kingdom of Ankole in southwestern Uganda was known not only for its long-horned cattle – as it still is – but also its absolute ruler, *mugabe* (king) who claimed that all the cattle in the land belonged to him. And the chiefs under him were ranked on the basis of how many cattle they had.

It was also a society divided on the basis of social classes. It was a kind of caste system although not as rigid as the one in India. The cattle owners, the Bahima, belonged to the higher class, and the Bairu farmers to the lower class.

And the country was excellent for livestock, with its rolling plains covered with abundant grass. But grazing land has diminished through the years because of high population growth.

The Banyankole are also known to be good story tellers. Riddles and proverbs are also very important in conversations and as a means to impart wisdom and teach the young their proper role in society. Combined with tales and legends, they also teach proper moral behaviour to the young. Of special significance are legends surrounding the institution of the kingship, which provide a historical framework for the Banyankole.

Although Christianity is prevalent, many Banyankole – including a significant number of Christians – pay a lot of attention to traditional secular and religious practices. The belief in ancestor spirits is very strong. Many Banyankole believe that if you neglect a dead realative, you incur the wrath of the ancestors. And an offering such as meat or milk must be offered to appease them.

In many respects, little has changed since the good old days especially in terms of customs and traditions mainly in the rural areas.

Like all other Africans in pre-colonial times, the Banyankole were an independent people. As Ghanaian philosopher Willie Abraham says, independence is a state of nature.

But the coming of Europeans changed all that. It signalled the beginning of the end of independence for the Banyankole and for the people of other kingdoms in Uganda.

The British signed a treaty with Ankole in 1894 and proclaimed the kingdom a British protectorate, ending independence for this traditional kingdom. It was a blow to these proud people.

The Banyankole strongly resisted British domination but were no match for imperial might. Crushed by British troops sent from Kenya and other nearby colonies ruled by Britain, the Banyankole were forced to sign an agreement with the colonial rulers which led to the formal incorporation of their kingdom into the Uganda Protectorate.

During the 1920s and 1930s, the colonial rulers greatly reduced the power of the Ankole king, the *omugabe*, and the political independence of the Ankole kingdom.

The British rulers were unpopular in Ankole. And they were more concerned about reaping economic benefits than with meeting the demands and aspirations of the people including preservation of traditional institutions – as well as the power and trappings of the monarchy – on terms stipulated by Ankole leaders. The Banyankole were a conquered people, reduced to a vast pool of cheap labour for the colonial rulers.

Ankole was less developed than other parts of the Uganda Protectorate and resentment against British rule fuelled Ankole nationalism during World War II, leading to the growth of a vibrant Ankole nationalist movement.

Opposition to British rule was not confined to Ankole. It became widespread in the southern part of the protectorate which was predominantly the land of kingdoms. As James Minahan states in the *Encyclopedia of the Stateless Nations*:

"The kingdoms of southern Uganda increasingly opposed inclusion in Uganda as the British territory moved toward independence in the decade after World War II.

The growing opposition to domination by Uganda's non-Bantu northern tribes pushed the Hima, Iru and Chiga to bury old differences and begin to identity with Ankole nationalism.

In the late 1950s, agitation for autonomy or separate independence swept the kingdom, but after extensive negotiations the Ankole finally accepted semifederal status within independent Uganda.

The independence government of Milton Obote, a non-Bantu northerner installed as Uganda's first president in 1962, quickly moved to curtail the powers of the southern kingdoms, over vehement Bantu opposition.

In 1966, amid growing tension and moves toward secession, the Obote government ended all Ankole autonomy and in 1967 abolished the four kingdoms." - (James Minahan, *Encyclopedia of the Stateless Nations: S-Z*, Westport, Connecticut, USA: Greenwood Publishing Group, 2002, p.132).

Abolition of the kingdoms galvanised opposition to Obote's rule among southern Ugandans and was a major factor in encouraging them to form an alliance in pursuit of a common goal.

They wanted to reclaim the power the kingdoms enjoyed before the advent of colonial rule. They also wanted a federal form of government in which they would enjoy autonomy and exercise considerable power in the context of a united Uganda if they could not secede. And they wanted Obote out of power.

The opportunity to get rid of Obote came in 1971 in a coup led by a fellow northerner, Idi Amin:

"Firmly opposed to the Obote government, most Ankole supported the revolt, led by Idi Amin Dada, that overthrew Obote in (January) 1971. Quickly disillusioned with the mercurial Dada, whose administration became even more repressive than Obote's, the Ankole withdrew their support.

Following an abortive secessionist revolt in 1972, Dada loosed his mainly Muslim army on Ankole (he was a Muslim himself). Thousands died in brutal massacres, and refugees streamed across the borders into Zaire and Rwanda.

Its leadership decimated, murdered, or disappeared, the Ankole national movement collapsed.

Idi Amin Dada, one of Africa's most brutal dictators, was finally overthrown in April 1979 and fled the country, but several successor governments lasted only short periods until Milton Obote again became president of

Uganda in 1980.

The Ankole, with vivid memories of Obote's earlier rule, gave their support to a southern Bantu rebel movement led by an ethnic Ankole Hima, Yoweri Museveni. The rebels drove Obote from office in 1986 and installed Museveni as the head of Uganda's first Bantu-dominated government." (Ibid.).

The insurgency was launched from Buganda which became the main operational base for the offensive against Obote's regime for strategic reasons. The seat of the national government was Kampala which is located in Buganda. The kingdom is centrally located. And the Baganda constitute the largest and most influential ethnic group in Uganda.

Museveni and his colleagues in the rebel movement were aware of all that. In fact, most of the support for the military operations by the insurgents came from the Baganda. They also provided the largest number of fighters. And Museveni promised them to restore their kingdom once he seized power.

After he seized power in January 1986, he restored peace and stability, which made him popular in many parts of the country, especially in the south, the ethnic stronghold of his fellow Bantus, except in the north, the homeland of both Obote and Amin.

But he still wanted even more support and also to consolidate his position as the nation's supreme leader. And his promise to re-institute the kingdoms was a tactical manoeuvre to help him achieve this goal.

Restoration of the kingdoms was a strategic decision that was brilliantly executed by Museveni and his colleagues in the government.

But it was also a strategic gamble which could backfire by fostering and fuelling regionalism and separatism – as well as secessionist tendencies – among some people in all the traditional kingdoms. And it did in a number of cases in varying degrees.

It also offended many northerners who were already opposed to his rule and who saw the restoration of the kingdoms as a nefarious scheme by Bantus to establish and perpetuate their hegemonic control of the country to the detriment of non-Bantu northerners who are predominantly Nilotic.

But the re-institution of the kingdoms also had unintended consequences for President Museveni and his government:

"Relative peace since 1986 has, paradoxically, allowed Ankole nationalism to resurface even though firmly opposed by President Museveni.

Led by the more militant Protestant minority (the majority of the Banyankole are Catholic), the nationalist movement is buoyed by nostalgia for the former monarchy and the memories of the peace and prosperity the kingdom enjoyed until 1967.

Ankole nationalism is sustained by the belief that an independent Ankole would have been spared the horrors and desolation of the years since 1962.

In 1992 the Ugandan government announced a radical decentralization of government, transferring power to councils in local areas, prompting calls for the restoration of the Ankole kingdom.

In July 1993 a new law restored all the former Bantu kingdoms except for Ankole.

Firmly opposed to the restoration of the Ankole kingdom, President Museveni refused to listen to Ankole arguments.

In November 1993, in defiance of the president, John Barigye was crowned king, and the restoration of the kingdom declared.

The proclamation, declared illegal by the Museveni government, set off a serious crisis between the Ankole government, backed by the nationalists, and Uganda's central government.

The Bantu majority of Ankole support restoration of the monarchy as a means of safeguarding their unique culture but have refused to consider the restoration of the Hima institutions of domination that formerly were an integral part of the monarchy.

In February 2000, President Museveni stated that he would consider the restoration of the monarchy if the majority of the people in the concerned districts demanded it.

The Nkore Cultural Trust (NCT), a pro-monarchy organization, began consulting leading members of the Ankole community about the delayed process of restoring the Ankole monarchy.

Nationalists want the restoration of the monarchy partly for tradition but also to unite the Ankole people, as politics and religion have failed to do.

The Ankole remain bitterly divided over the future of their homeland. Some want a restoration of the kingdom and autonomy or independence. Others, mostly non-Ankole, but also many Ankole, in the outer areas of the old kingdom, reject the monarchy but support greater autonomy.

In 2001 nationalists proposed the creation of a new Ankole to include the Ankole-populated districts of Mbarara, Bushenyi, and Ntungamo. Nationalists also claim the Rujumbura and Rubado counties of Rukungiri District, which is inhabited by ethnic Ankole.

Economic and political instability in the Great Lakes region of Africa has fueled the growth of Ankole nationalism. The prohibition on political organizations in Uganda and a lack of even the traditional democratic traditions of the Ankole kingdom makes nationalism an attractive alternative to many young Ankole.

The largest nationalist organization, the Banyankore Cultural Foundation (BCF), although openly nationalist, rejects the monarchy as an antiquated caste system that divided Ankole into classes or castes. Reviving the monarchy, according to the group, means reviving social injustice and endangering the unity that has been growing in Ankole." - (Ibid., pp. 132 – 133; Samwiri Ruharaza Karugire, *A History of the Kingdom of Nkore in Western Uganda to 1896*, Fountain Publishers, 1971; Martin R. Doornbos, *Not All the King's Men: Inequality as A Political Instrument in Ankole, Uganda (Change and Continuity in Africa)*, Mouton, 1978; Ramkrishna Mukherjee, *Uganda: An Historical Accident, Class, Nation, State Formation*, Africa World Press, 1985; Francis A.W. Bwengye, *The Agony of Uganda, from Idi Amin to Obote: Repressive Rule and Bloodshed: Causes, Effects, and the Cure*, London & New York: Regency Press,1985).

Among the Banyankole, the quest for the restoration of the Ankole kingdom is not only fuelled by nostalgia for the past but also by contemporary necessities in the political and economic realms.

It's the only former kingdom which has not regained its former status. But it may also be the only kingdom in Uganda where a significant number of people don't want to re-institute the monarchy while at the same time retaining pride in their political and cultural achievements and ethnic identity.

And as these groups – traditionalists versus modernists including a combination of both – vie for leadership and influence in Ankole, they have been equally adept at seeking government assistance to promote their agendas for the benefit of their people as a whole especially in the economic arena where competition between them for resources would be to the detriment of the Ankole as a collective entity.

Also, the refusal by President Museveni to restore the kingdom's former status should not be misconstrued as anti-Ankole. He's Ankole himself. But many Ankole are adamant in their demand for the restoration of the Ankole kingdom in one form or another.

And as Yoga Adhola, former editor-in-chief of *The People* newspaper of the Uganda People's Congress (UPC) which was Obote's ruling party, stated in his Op-Ed in the *Sunday Monitor*, Kampala, Uganda, entitled "Ankole Kingdom Was Also Conquered":

"There is something weird about President Museveni's perspective of history. It has tendencies to select either a phase of history or particular sections of history and go on to act as if that is the whole history.

He acts as though the causes of the issues he deals with begin with independence. He does not delve into the historical circumstances which led to those issues. It therefore becomes very easy for him to set up caricatures and treat them as real issues.

In his recent history lesson again he was selective. He argued that the kingdoms of Bunyoro, Buganda and Tooro were conquered by Luos, and then went on to make the claim that since the Luos did not reach Ankole, Ankole was never conquered.

But at the very time in history that President Museveni says the Babito conquered Buganda, Bunyoro and Tooro, the Bahima also arrived in present day Ankole. They found indigenous people there, subjugated them and now call them Bairus.

Unlike the Luos who got assimilated into their respective societies, the Bahima established a ruthless caste system which survives today. The caste system was marked by race and certain prohibitions.

The Bahima depended for their livelihoods on cattle while the Bairu on agriculture. The Bairu were not permitted to own productive cows. If a Mwiru came to possess a productive cow, any Muhima had the right to take it from him.

The Bairu were not allowed to marry Hima girls yet

100

Hima boys could take Bairu girls for concubines.

The Bairu were barred from military service and no Mwiru could hold high official positions. Furthermore, they had no political status.

The Bahima organised and evolved a state apparatus. Centred around the Omugabe (king), the Hima state provided protection against foreign aggression and also subordinated the Bairu.

When the British came, they merely refashioned the Hima state and, through the system of indirect rule, used it to run this part of the colony. Thus British colonialism, entrenched Hima domination.

As time went on, colonialism occasioned social development that undermined social stratification along caste lines.

'The effect of modern education was to instill egalitarian orientations and aspirations among an increasing number of Bairu giving rise to a growing sense of dissatisfaction over their status as second class citizens.

Bairu also developed an awareness of greater self-sufficiency from this mastery of modern skills, as well as from new sources of income made available to them through the cultivation and sale of cash crops.'

This led Bairu to demand for equality, particularly following the Second World War. The late 1940s was a period of very intense struggles at Mbarara High School between the Hima and Bairu students. It was as a result of these struggles that an organisation of Bairus called Kumanyana to articulate Bairu interests was formed.

One of the greatest achievements of Kumanyana was the election of Kesi Nganwa as the Engazi (Chief Minister) of Ankole. Nganwa was the first Mwiru to hold that post, and his election was very uplifting to the Bairus. They gave him the title of Ruterengwa which means nothing compares with him. The Hima strongly objected to this because it implied that Nganwa was of higher status than the Omugabe.

The rise of NRM has essentially restored the status of the Bahima. It has done so not just in Ankole, but extended it to the rest of Uganda." - (Yoga Adhola, "Ankole Kingdom Was Also Conquered," *Sunday Monitor*, Kampala, Uganda, 20 April 2008).

The logic for the restoration of the kingdoms may be convoluted, according to some people, and is probably best exemplified by President Museveni himself. But it serves the president well as part of his Machiavellian tactics to rule Uganda and perpetuate himself in power until he's ready to step down on his own terms. As Machiavelli says, "It's better to be feared than loved." In the case of Museveni, it's also better to be complex and divisive and confuse your opponents than please them.

The people of Ankole also use the vote and political support as a bargaining tool in an attempt to extract concessions from the government and have threatened to withhold their support if they don't get what they want.

They also demand their share of the economic pie, not only as Ugandans but as a people who collectively constitute one of the four major kingdoms in the country which lost their powers during colonial rule and even their status as kingdoms under President Obote. According to a report in the *Uganda Heritage News*:

"The Ankole Cultural group is demanding president Museveni to extend kingdom facilitation to their area. President Museveni recently offered 4 billion shillings to the kingdoms of Busoga, Bunyoro and Buganda.

Moses Kanaala, the chairman of Ankole Cultural Group says that Museveni should not be discriminative but extend the kingdom facilitation to all tribes, districts and races found in Uganda.

Although there is no recognized kingdom in Ankole region, Kanaala reminds Museveni that Ankole was a full kingdom under Omugabe in the written history of Uganda and so the president should not forget to extend kingdom facilitation to them.

Kanaala says the people of Ankole would not give Museveni support come 2011 if the president doesn't extend financial facilitation to Ankole Cultural Group. Kanaala says Ankole Cultural Group is a registered cultural association under the rules and procedures in the laws of Uganda.

Kanaala says the ultimate goal of Ankole Cultural Group is to have Ankole kingdom restored. Kanaala claims that it's president Museveni frustrating the restoration of Ankole kingdom." - ("Ankole Cultural Groups Demands Kingdom Facilitation," *Uganda Heritage News*, 22 April 2009).

The demand for the restoration of the kingdom is supported even by some of the most ardent Ugandan nationalists among the Banyankole who are committed to maintaining the territorial integrity of Uganda as a single nation. They don't see any contradiction between the two. And they are committed to achieving both.

The debate over the status of the kingdoms is a divisive issues among many Ugandans in different parts of the country. And it may not end until all the kingdoms regain their former status even if with diminished influence in terms of political power.

And they all have been accorded that status except Ankole, even though there are still some demands from all the kingdoms which have not been met by the government.

Full restoration of political power, and the establishment of a federal form of government with extensive devolution of power to the kingdoms and the regions, are the biggest demands which have not yet been met. And they probably never will in the context of modern Uganda.

But that has not stifled nationalist aspirations at the

micro-national level in the kingdoms which in many ways still see themselves as nations, as they indeed once were during pre-colonial times, regardless of how anachronistic they may be in the context of the modern African state which eschews and transcends ethnicity.

And among all the kingdoms, the most vocal demands come from Ankole because it has not been allowed to regain its former status as a traditional kingdom. But there is still hope because many Banyankole have not lost hope. According to a report in the *Monitor*, Kampala, Uganda, "The Man Who Would Be King from Ankole":

"On the early afternoon of January 8, 2008, Prince John Barigye, heir to the Ankole throne, sat down to discuss his hope – or the lack of it – that the kingdom will carry on into the next generation.

In intermittent telephone conversations with friends, held between answering my questions, he mentioned that he was working hard to improve his health and stay fit.

Two days later, on January 10, it would be his 68th birthday, more than 15 years after his 1993 enthronement was nullified by President Yoweri Museveni.

It is what they call patience, Prince Barigye said, yet only when he said that he had been crown prince since he was 13, a student at King's College (Budo), did the full extent of his endurance sink in.

His story, as glorious as it is painful, takes you from Kampala to New York, from Lusaka to Rome – a convoluted journey that even he struggled to recount accurately.

The ultimate glory, of course, has not come, but the portly prince never came across as a whiner, choosing instead to portray himself as an aristocrat who trusts more in the clarity of his conscience than the comfort to be found in bashing his detractors.

Yes, Prince Barigye showed no signs of an angry man, showing little or no sentiment about issues that he holds

104

dear, especially the question of the confiscated royal drums of Ankole.

Although some critics have speculated that the drums are being kept at State House, an allegation that the prince himself seemed to back in a past interview, he told me that all of the kingdom's regalia has been left to rot inside an underground chamber of the Uganda Museum.

The royal drums, including the lead drum (bagyendanwa), traditionally were the ultimate symbol of Ankole power, and it is said that the reigning monarch is powerful only if he has access to the drums.

'As a matter of fact, in 1993 we received a communication from State House...[telling] us categorically that the royal drums would be handed over to us, and they instructed the Ministry of Tourism and Antiquities to allow us inspect them with a view to handing over the drums and other regalia to us,' he said, recalling that visit to the Uganda Museum revealed that the drums 'were in a bad state, just thrown about.'

Pleas to let the royal family keep the drums, which go back to the days of the Bachwezi (1300 to 1500 AD), fell on deaf ears, Prince Barigye said, insisting that the drums are family property.

'We, only us, know how to look after those things. They belong to us, and they have been with us for centuries,' he said.

'Whether the Ankole Kingdom is restored or not, those drums are actually our property.'

On November 20, 1993, Crown Prince John Patrick Barigye Rutashijuka Ntare VI was crowned as Omugabe at a secret ceremony that was said to have been a conspiracy between certain senior army officers and monarchists, but was without the backing of President Museveni's administration.

The coronation was not as secretive as it should have been, and news of the ceremony leaked and led Mr Museveni to quickly annul the enthronement.

Prince Barigye has since lived in relative obscurity, staying away from controversy and rarely giving interviews about the state of his kingdom. In reality, he is a prince who might never be king, a monarch who exists essentially in name.

Those who opposed his coronation, including prominent members of the Museveni administration, argued that his enthronement would be a throwback to the days of ethnic tension between the Bairu and Bahima sub-tribes of Ankole.

Blocking the restoration of Ankole's kingship, Mr Museveni announced that the institution's future, and with it that of the royal family, would be determined by the people of Ankole.

There has never been a referendum to determine just how popular the idea is, and most opposition to the kingship has been premised on the popular perception that the Bairu, who make up the bulk of Ankole, do not support a kingship that is likely to resurrect Bahima dominance.

So, while the existence of a kingdom in Ankole could not be plagued by legal uncertainties, its restoration remains a fleeting dream, leaving critics to postulate that Mr Museveni – who comes from Ankole and is a Muhima – just could not come to terms with the idea of a rival centre of power in his backyard.

'What does one mean if he says the people of Ankole should decide? It is not consistent [with] what has happened in other parts of Uganda, nor is it a requirement of the law,' Prince Barigye said.

Prince Barigye's father, Rutahaba Gasyonga II, the last *de facto* Omugabe of Ankole, died in 1979, some 12 years after President Milton Obote's abolition of cultural institutions.

Since then, even though the Traditional Institutions Statute of 1993 restored kingdoms, Ankole is still waiting for its cultural leader.

But Prince Barigye did not agree entirely, arguing that

'the Banyankole installed me as king of Ankole despite the protestations of a number of very influential people in the central government who were not in favour of the institution.'

Prince Barigye's viewpoint, it would seem, is based more on the conviction that the government may refuse to recognise his status, but it can never be able to undo his enthronement.

'Many people in Ankole and other parts of Uganda recognise me as the Omugabe of Ankole,' he said. 'To them who recognise me as the Omugabe, the institution exists. It has been the hope of those attached to this institution all these years that the government will reach a position when it could change its views.'

Arguing that Ankole had been treated differently, Prince Barigye reasoned that the Banyankole who 'wish' to unite under a cultural institution should not be denied.

'There is no one who can say that in Ankole there are not a significant number of people who are not attached to the monarchy,' he said, adding that nowhere in Uganda have cultural institutions found universal acceptance.

'Of course, there are people in Ankole who don't want a monarchy. But you find the same pattern in every part [of Uganda] where a monarchy existed before.'

An institution called Nkore Cultural Trust (NCT), whose original goal was to lobby the central government to recognise the Ankole kingship, today exists to manage the affairs of the kingdom.

One thing, though, is for sure – NCT is yet to get hold of the royal drums, in state custody since 1967.

In fact, as Prince Barigye said, all the worthy royal jewels remain in the hands of the central government.

'If [the drums] are kept because some people don't want the Kingdom of Ankole back, why not give them to us who value them? Why leave them to rot away? It's a bit like the biblical story of the two women who were fighting for a child,' he said.

Rose Nkaale, the Uganda Museum curator, said the royal drums of Ankole, and other regalia associated with the kingdom, are still in their custody.

'We are conserving the drums, [but] they are not on display. They are in our strong room....Until we get authorisation from State House, we cannot display [the items]," she said recently.

Asked why such authorisation had to come from State House, the official residence of the President of Uganda, Ms Nkaale modified her answer, saying instead that she meant 'the government.' Ms Nkaale did not reveal the precise location of the Ankole regalia.

Mwambutsya Ndebesa, a Makerere University historian, said the only sure thing about the drums is that 'the Obote government took them to the National Museum' after the 1967 abolition of traditional institutions. '[Now] they could be somewhere else,' Mr Ndebesa said in a recent interview.

Prince Barigye refused to blame Mr Museveni, maintaining that while the Ankole affair has become a political one, he does not believe that Mr Museveni is implacably opposed to the Ankole kingship or that the royal drums are now kept somewhere in State House!

Even when he launched into some of the most painful details of his royal odyssey, Prince Barigye was not one to show some passion, forcing me to ask him just why he had chosen not to do battle; to fight for what he considers his inheritance.

Did his apparent resignation come naturally for him or was it deliberate?

'Well, the institution is not my personal property,' he said, adding that he takes umbrage on behalf of his followers.

'It is not for me to speak up passionately for the institution; it's for the people who are attached to it to speak out.'

Today's monarchy is not modelled on the one of yore,

Prince Barigye said, seemingly hard-pressed to see why the central government would not recognise his kingship.

The Bahima-Bairu card is not strong enough to forever kill the Ankole kingship, he said.

'I could understand that argument if we were talking about the monarchy of the old days, when the kings had political power. But the kings now don't have political, judicial or any legislative powers; they are purely cultural,' he said.

Prince Barigye today leads the life of a retiree, as he put it. If he is not at his palace in Rubindi in Mbarara, where he spends half his time herding his cattle, he could be entertaining guests, writing, or running his businesses.

'I am basically retired, although I am still active,' he said.

But I still wanted to know whether, from his perspective, the case for the Ankole kingship is as strong as it was, say, in 1993.

Had he really given up? Was cynicism catching up with him?

'You should ask the people who are attached to the monarchy,' he said, his face breaking into a chuckle.

'But I would say [that] the kingdom of Ankole, and indeed all those areas where they have had kings, is the embodiment of the history and identity of the people.'

In the years that the Ankole kingship has taken a beating, Prince Barigye claimed, the 'culture of our people has suffered a lot. The young people have no point of reference, no point of guidance. They behave in any way they want, and you see it in many aspects. It is a loss of bearing.'

Listening to Prince Barigye's diplomatic tone, I was left wondering if his tenor would have been different had I met him in a room rarefied by old photographs from days gone by, a place with reminders of what would have been, perhaps a place like his own home.

We met inside the lobby of a Kampala restaurant of his

choice, where classical music brought a genteel atmosphere to the air, where maids walking by presented the occasional distraction, where the ambience is not what you would find inside Prince Barigye's palace.

But when he recited his résumé, there was enough evidence to suggest that his diplomacy with the government was not a charade, that his answers were not contrived, and that he was a man for whom life's joys trumped its miseries.

Born on January 10, 1940, Prince Barigye was educated at King's College, Cambridge, where he studied economics.

On return to a soon-to-be-independent Uganda, he had a stint in the Ministry of Commerce before joining the Ministry of Foreign Affairs, where he rose through the ranks to the position of permanent secretary during the first Obote administration.

In the early years of Idi Amin's presidency, Prince Barigye was Uganda's ambassador to the Federal Republic of Germany and, later, to the Vatican.

On a visit to Uganda in 1969, Pope Paul VI knighted Prince Barigye, who in 1973 resigned from government, citing Amin's brutality.

'I went into exile and lived in Zambia. I had to start afresh, just like a university graduate,' he said of his time at the Industrial Development Corporation of Zambia.

'But again I rose through the ranks, and by the time I left them I was a manager...'

Later, in 1979, Prince Barigye accepted to be a senior regional trade policy advisor at the United Nations Conference on Trade and Development, covering all the English-speaking developing countries in Africa – 'a job I did not even apply for.'

When his contract expired, about four years later, Prince Barigye ran his own businesses in Lesotho, and did not return to Uganda until 1986 when President Museveni took power after a five year guerrilla war.

In 1989, he was elected to represent Kashari in the National Resistance Council, the day's legislature, serving in that role until it became apparent that all kingdoms in existence before 1967 would be restored.

Prince Barigye has almost been everything – from businessman to legislator to diplomat – but his impressive résumé remains incomplete: officially, he is not king of the Banyankole." - (Rodney Muhumuza, "The Man Who Would Be King from Ankole," *Monitor*, Kampala, Uganda, 21 September 2008).

Many Banyankole may have accepted fate and probably believe that their glorious past can not be reclaimed and relived in the form of a restored kingdom. But there are still many others who believe that there are better days ahead.

They look to the future of a reinvigorated past, a golden era of cultural revival and pride even if they may never again enjoy the political power they once had during the good ol' days before the advent of imperial rule.

Another well-known traditional political and cultural grouping in Uganda is the princedom of Busoga which is also one of the most prominent ethnic entities in the Great Lakes region of East Africa.

The Basoga are organised on the basis of clans, a common feature in many traditional societies across the continent. They're also closely related to the Baganda and the Banyoro as well other Bantu ethnic groups in Uganda and across the border in Kenya.

Most of the people are farmers. And the vast majority of them grow crops on small farms for their own consumption.

The main commercial crops are sugar cane and tea. They are grown on plantations.

Other crops include bananas, maize, millet, rice, sweet potatoes, fruits and vegetables.

The northern part of Busoga is known for its cattle and

111

other domesticated animals including sheep and goats. It also supports agriculture. But the region, especially Kamuli District, is known for its cattle more than anything else and is a part of the cattle corridor of East Africa.

The people of Busoga are known as Basoga – singular Musoga. And they speak Lusoga, a Bantu language. It evolved from a combination of several dialects to become one of the most prominent local languages in Uganda. It's related to Lunyoro and Luganda.

The origin of the Basoga also is inextricably linked with the origin of other Bantu groups who trace their roots to what's now Congo and before then West Africa, especially what's now Cameroon and eastern Nigeria.

It's believed that the earliest inhabitants of the region that's now Busoga were the Langi who today are – together with the Acholi – one of the main ethnic groups in northern Uganda. The Iteso and the Bagishu or Bagisu also preceded the Basoga in what's now Busoga. And the Basoga were later overwhelmed by the Baganda.

Besides the Baganda and the Banyoro as the founders of the Busoga kingdom (princedom), there was another major Bantu group which played a role in the establishment of this traditional entity. They were the Banyankole. They're are said to be some of the earliest settlers in Busoga who occupied the shore areas near Lake Victoria and were later joined by other people from the Mount Elgon area.

Other people from different parts of what's now western Kenya also migrated into the area during those early years.

The impact of all these outside influences has been profound on the evolution of Busoga in terms of ethnic composition, linguistic development, and cultural fusion:

"Originally, the Basoga were a disunited people. They could not unite even in the face of a common enemy. This explains why they were incessantly prone to foreign influence, first from Bunyoro and later from Buganda.

Language

Lusoga language closely approximates to Luganda, especially that spoken by the Ssese islanders.

There exist many Lusoga dialects. However, Buganda influence over Busoga was so much that Luganda tends to be used as a lingua franca in Busoga more than Lusoga itself.

Within Busoga, there are so many dialects of the Lusoga language that it is difficult to reach agreement on the correct way to spell or pronounce certain words. For instance, in the north of Busoga, there is a distinct H but people from southern Busoga do not accept this H as being appropriate to the Lusoga Language.

Luo influences

The Basoga were also under the influence of the Luo rulers of Bunyoro. As a result, the Basoga followed some of the Luo customs. For example, at puberty they used to extract the sixth teeth in the lower jaw as initiation adulthood like the Alur of West Nile and the Joluo of western Kenya. Even some of their ceremonies especially those regarding death, tended to resemble those of the Luo.

Land ownership and the economy

In Busoga, each clan had land and the *mutaka* (clan head) was responsible for the clan's land. This land could not pass ownership from one clan to another nor could a member who was granted land by the clan head be deprived of it. There was plenty of land in spite the population. Any member could get land by simply asking the clan head for it.

A non-clan member could be allowed to cultivate land but only as a *mugiha* (tenant). The land could be taken from him if it was required by any member of the clan to which it belonged.

They were settled agriculturalists and they were quite rich in food and cattle.

Death and burial rites:

A chief

Whenever an important chief was sick, very few people were allowed to come near him.

His death was first kept a secret until all his wives, cattle, hoes, ivory, and male slaves had been secured.

Thereafter, the official announcement was made early in the morning by *a mujwa* (funeral officer). It was then that the chief's wives, herdsmen, and people wept and kissed the corpse.

No work of any kind could be done, not even visiting or cooking could be done. If there happened to be any other dead people, their burials had to wait until the chief's funeral rites were completed.

It was taboo for any cock to crow during the period. No one shaved until the rites were over. The older wives of the chief were gathered and kept in the death hut for seven days supporting the body of the dead chief across their feet. For these days, they were not supposed to touch food of any kind.

Burial

The chief was buried in the hut of his first wife. He was buried with some objects, his body facing towards their supposed direction of origin.

Most Basoga bury their dead facing northward because they believe that they came from Bunyoro. The chief's grave was deep indeed about ten metres.

Before burial, the corpse was washed all over by the wives. A new bark cloth was hung across the doorway of the hut. The corpse was smeared with butter and a large coloured bead was tied around the neck.

In Bugabula, a piece of flayed cow-hide was taken from a cow sacrificed to the dead and laid upon the forehead of the corpse.

Other presents like beads, wires or bracelets were also tied on the arms and legs of the corpse. The body was then carried to the burial hut by the Bwagwa and put in the grave but no earth was put in yet. A bullock was tied to the doorway of the hut and dedicated to the dead chief. The ceremony was extended to inaugurate an heir.

Burial of the head of the family

All children kissed the corpse and wailed loudly. No cooking was allowed for one day.

His grave could be dug in his own hut, garden or courtyard. The heir could be appointed at the time of burial.

The other rites were not reopened to add fresh barkcloths like the chief's. They could only sprinkle beer and blood over the grave.

Burial of a childless man

A young man was treated like an old man. If he was unmarried, a widower, or married but without children, a broom was placed on the grave and he was ordered not to come back in the following words: 'Go straight away and never return to earth, you childless one.'

His name was despised in the society and care was taken not to give it to another person for fear that he also might become childless.

Burial of a married woman

The husband would wail and kiss the corpse and so would some relatives. She was buried in the banana plantations according to the customs of the husband.

Often, she was made to lie on her left. She was informed upon being buried that none of those present had caused her death and was implored not to comeback for revenge.

Should she have possessed property, her spirit was placated by the offer of a goat or a bullock before the heir took over the property.

Customs demanded that the dead woman's relatives should bring forward an unmarried girl and give her to the dead woman's husband. This girl became the heiress and took over the functions and property of the dead woman.

If the deceased woman had daughters who were married, their husbands had to redeem them from the deaths spirits with a goat.

There was another special ceremony for a dead woman who left married sons. Each of the wives of her sons cooked food and took it to the burial where they would find their husbands awaiting them.

If the deceased woman had daughters who were married, their husbands had to redeem them from the deaths spirits with a goat.

The women dressed themselves up like men and went to the banana plantations. They would sit down in a manner men did when they went to arrange the bride wealth or to redeem their wives from funeral rites.

Their husbands would dress up like women and come to greet their wives. Then they would do all they could to make their wives laugh. If any of the women laughed, she was deemed unfit; the food she brought was considered unfit for eating; and her marriage was cancelled.

In case of a childless woman, the speaker said, 'Never

116

come back for you left nothing behind.'

A broom was then placed on the grave and her name was allowed to die out of society.

Unmarried girls were buried in almost the same way as women, only no heiress was necessary.

Religion

The Basoga believed in the existence of a spirit world. They called the Supreme Being *Lubaale*.

Human agents worked as messengers of Lubaale, or the ancestors, or other minor gods.

To the Basoga, the spirit world, places of worship, animated objects and fetishes had power to do good or evil to the living.

The Basoga call magicians, fetishmen and spirit mediums *Bachwezi*.

The Basoga believed in the existence of gods and sub-gods.

Below *Lubaale*, there were *Mukama* the creator of all things; *Jingo*, the public god who attended to the general needs of the people; *Nawandyo*; and *Bilungo* the god of plagues.

Semanda, Gasani and *Kitaka* were other gods the Basoga believed in.

Political set-up

There were no paramount chief over the whole of Busoga. The Basoga were organised into principalities or chiefdoms under the sovereignty of Bunyoro and later Buganda.

In early times, the death of a chief was first reported to the Omukama of Bunyoro who would send the funeral barkcloth and all the necessary requirements for the burial rites.

On several occasions, he used to appoint the heir or

117

send back the son of the deceased chief if the son happened, as usually the case, to be at the Mukama's court in Bunyoro.

During the time of the Luo migration, Luo sub-dynasties were established in Busoga. Among these sub-dynasties (at lest six in all), Bukoli and Bugwere were founded about the same time as the Babiito dynasty of Bunyoro at the beginning of the 16th century.

By the turn of the 19th century, there were fifteen virtually independent principalities. In fact, the southern principalities are said to have been ruled by dynasties whose origins could be traced to the east and Lake Victoria islands.

During the 19th century, Buganda influence very greatly increased over the southern Busoga principalities.

The northern principalities still had a connection with Bunyoro and indeed their language contained Runyoro words.

In 1906, the British protectorate accomplished an administrative amalgamation of the multifarious kingdoms of pre-colonial Busoga into a single integrated structure. Representatives from the small pre-colonial kingdoms consisted of the Busoga Lukiiko.

In the same year Semei Kakungulu was appointed President of the Lukiiko. His reign ended with his resignation in 1913. This led to the collapse of the monstrous political structure and the abolition of the office of 'president of the Lukiiko of Busoga.'

Later, there arose demands within the Basoga for the revival of the office. In 1919 the Isembantu Kyabaziga office was established as an alternative to it. And Ezekeeri Wako was appointed the first Isebantu Kyabazinga." - ("Uganda Culture and People: The Busoga Culture, Origins, Legends, Religion, Political Setup").

Although Busoga was not as strong as Bunyoro or Buganda in terms of political power and military might, it was the most integrated traditional "kingdom" in terms of ethnic composition when the colonial rulers arrived.

It was a product of many ethnic groups and cultures. And its existence as an integrated society is strong testimony to the political genius of its founders and its people who have worked together through the decades to create one of the most cohesive traditional societies on the African continent.

The traditional homeland of the Basoga also has many tourist attractions. Their capital, Jinja, is not only one of the most important towns in Uganda and in the entire East Africa; it's also the source of the Nile.

It's at Jinja where River Nile starts to flow north out of Lake Victoria. And many people from many parts of the world visit Jinja every year. to see the source of the Nile.

But that's just one of the major attractions Busoga has. Its strategic location alone on the shores of Lake Victoria is enough to draw countless visitors every year and is a major asset to Uganda.

Other major Bantu groups in Uganda – besides the Baganda, Banyoro, Batoro and Basoga – include the Bakiga and the Bagisu.

The Bakiga live mostly in Kabale District – which once was a part of the larger Kigezi District before it was split up – in southwestern Uganda. They straddle the Ugandan-Rwandan border and also live in northwestern Rwanda. They're sometimes called northern Hutus.

They migrated to Uganda from what's now Rwanda between 1600s and 1700s.

They have also migrated to other parts of Uganda because of overpopulation in their homeland in the southwestern part of the country.

And this has led to conflict with other ethnic groups including their neighbours such as the Banyoro and those much farther away such as the Baganda. According to a report in a government-owned newspaper, *New Vision*, Kampala, Uganda, "Banyoro-Bakiga Peace Talks to Begin

Soon, Says President," 11 February 2008:

"An investigation into the clashes between the Banyoro and Bakiga in Kibaale district is complete, President Yoweri Museveni has said.

The President was on Saturday speaking during the wedding reception of the lands state minister, Kasirivu Atwooki, at Kakoora village in Kibaale district.

Museveni said the probe committee that was established following the 2001 clashes had already submitted its report. The committee was led by Prof. Ruth Mukama.

The two ethnic groups have had a strained relationship for close to 15 years.

The President reassured the residents that contrary to some rumours that the Government had sidelined the issue, discussions between the Bakiga and Banyoro to resolve their differences would start 'with immediate effect.'

'We were delayed by the Commonwealth Heads of Government Meeting. We are going to sit and iron out this, to have harmony and peace in this area.'

In the 2001 local council elections, Fred Ruremera, a Mukiga won the LC5 seat, but was rejected by the Banyoro, leading to clashes.

Museveni later intervened and after negotiations with Ruremera, George William Namyaka, a Munyoro, was appointed chairperson.

Ruremera was sponsored for further studies.

Clashes again erupted in 2004, following the migration of more Bakiga into Kibaale.

In the 2006 polls, Namyaka stood unopposed, saving the district more bloodshed.

Museveni warned the Bakiga against undermining the Banyoro but also cautioned the latter against forgetting the tradition of the kingdom.

'Bunyoro has never been a one-tribe kingdom, and

should still embrace these fellow Ugandans,' he said.

Kasirivu, who had spent 20 years with his partner, Margaret Kyalisiima, walked her down the aisle at Blessed Trinity Catholic parish in Nalweyo, during a mass led by the Bishop of Hoima Diocese, the Rt. Rev Deogratius Byabazaire.

The President urged the minister to sustain the love for his wife.

Other notable guests included Bishop Emeritus Edward Baharagate, Bishop Stanley Ntagali of Masindi-Kitara Diocese, Omukama Solomon Gafabusa and FDC vice-chairperson Salaamu Musumba.

Meanwhile, Museveni has revealed that the Government would finance projects in six families per parish under the Prosperity-for-All (Bonna Bagaggawale) programme that will act as role models." - (Conan Businge, "Banyoro-Bakiga Peace Talks to Begin Soon, Says President," *New Vision*, Kampala, Uganda, 11 February 2008).

The inter-tribal or inter-ethnic conflicts over land raises serious questions about national unity and identity. Do members of different ethnic groups see themselves as fellow Ugandans first, or does their ethnic identity take precedence over national identity?

It seems the majority of them consider themselves Banyoro, Bakiga, or Baganda. So do the rest. Their tribe comes first. That's also the case in Kenya, Rwanda and Burundi. Tanzania is the only exception among the East African countries where tribalism has virtually been conquered. As Tanzanian writer Godfrey Mwakikagile states:

"We may not have conquered tribalism in Tanzania, but we have been able to contain it effectively. And that's no mean achievement; a rare feat on a continent where the idea of nation as a transcendent phenomenon in a polyethnic context remains a nebulous concept." - (Godfrey Mwakikagile, *Ethnic Politics in Kenya and Nigeria*, Huntington, New York, Nova Science Publishers, Inc., 2001, p. 234).

And as black American writer Keith Richburg who was bureau chief of *The Washington Post* in East Africa, based in Nairobi, Kenya, in the 1990s, states in his book *Out of America: A Black Man Confronts Africa*:

"One of my earliest trips was to Tanzania, and there I found a country that had actually managed to purge itself of the evil of tribalism.

Under Julius Nyerere..., the government was able to imbue a true sense of nationalism that transcended the country's natural ethnic divisions, among other things by vigorous campaigns to upgrade education and to make Swahili a truly national language....

Tanzania is one place that has succeeded in removing the linguistic barrier that separates so many of Africa's warring factions.

But after three years traveling the continent, I've found that Tanzania is the exception, not the rule. In Africa..., it *is* all about tribes." - Keith B. Richburg, *Out of America: A Black Man Confronts Africa*, New York, Basic Books, Harper-Collins, 1998, p. 240. See also Godfrey Mwakikagile, *Nyerere and Africa: End of an Era*, Fourth Edition, Pretoria, South Africa, 2008, pp. 507, and 735; G. Mwakikagile, *Ethnic Politics in Kenya and Nigeria*, op.cit., p. 234).

The tribal conflicts over land – and over anything else – are symptomatic of a much deeper problem: the inability and unwillingness to transcend tribal loyalties and rivalries for the sake of national unity. Many people simply refuse to accept each other as equals and as fellow citizens in spite of their common identity as Ugandans.

122

The politics of ethnicity even acquired the stamp of "legitimacy" when a few years earlier some members of parliament also blamed the Bakiga for "grabbing" land which belonged to the Baganda and other ethnic groups. According to a report in *New Vision*, "MP Attacks Bakiga for Grabbing Buganda Land-Bukedde":

"An MP stunned fellow MPs by charging that the hospitality practised by the Baganda towards other ethnic groups has been so passive that it has led other tribes to turn against them by robbing them of their land. In this connection, he did single out the Bakiga and accused them of robbing land in Mubende, Kayunga and in other parts of Buganda.

Rev. Kefa Sempagi, MP for Ntenjeru South was contributing to a parliamentary debate on a report by the Uganda Human Rights Commission on how various fundamental rights of Ugandans had been violated.

Hon. Rev. Sempagi went on to say that people had failed to honour the land-related law and just grabbed land that belonged to others. On this issue, he did point out the Bakiga whom he said first grabbed land in Sembabule and have now moved on to scramble for land in Mubende in what he referred to as a self-feasting spree.

He was supported by Rev. Peter Bakaluba Mukasa (Mukono North) who mentioned that the Bakiga had not stopped at Mubende but had gone on to invade land in Mukono and have settled in almost all the forests without following the legal procedures.

On his part, Rev. Sempagi told Parliament that the Baganda are kind people who have all along extended hospitality to other ethnic groups but that it is sad that those to whom due hospitality had been given have now turned against them by robbing them so as to turn them into squatters.

The MP (Ndorwa West) Stephen Bamwanga expressed his disapproval about the Bakiga having been painted negatively as robbers of land and called for a clarification as to whether there exists law that prohibits or restricts any Ugandan from settling anywhere as he/she wishes to. Rev. Sempala explained that the Bakiga he refers to are indeed land grabbers and named Katosi, Kiganda and a number of other places in Mubende that they had robbed.

However, Hon. Ben Wacha (Oyama North) did not take Sempagi's and Balukuba's allegations lightly and charged them for turning Parliament into a platform to spread ethnic hatred. He asked the Deputy Speaker Hon. Kadaga to caution both Hon. Sempagi and Hon. Balukuba, which she did." (Omar Kezimbira," MP Attacks Bakiga for Grabbing Buganda Land-Bukedde," *New Vision*, Kampala, Uganda, 12 December 2002).

Such ethnophobia has a tendency to spread and feed on itself. And it's highly contagious. It could destroy the social fabric of Uganda which holds the people together as a single nation with equal rights including the right to live wherever they want to live.

The Bakiga are only one group who have incurred the wrath of their fellow countrymen for moving into areas where they are not welcome and where they are seen as foreigners in their own country.

The Bakiga speak Rukiga, a Bantu language. And they share cultural traits – perhaps even biological ties – with the Banyambo of northwestern Tanzania. One theory even suggests that they migrated from Karagwe in what's now northwestern Tanzania. But historical evidence shows that the Bakiga who settled in southwestern Uganda came from northwestern neighbouring Rwanda.

Their social organisation is based on clans like that of many other African ethnic groups.

The biggest clan was the Basiga. Each clan was composed of several lineages and each lineage had a head known as *Omukuru w'omuryango*. A man was not allowed to marry from his clan.

Payment of dowry was an integral part of marriage arrangements. Usually cows, goats and hoes were given as dowry. And it was taboo to sell any animals given as bride wealth. Such animals could also be used to obtain wives for the girl's brothers or father.

Traditionally, the Bakiga are a very polygamous society. The number of wives is only limited by the availability of land and bride wealth obligations. That was especially the case in the past when polygamy was even more widespread. But it's an institution that's cherished even today as much as it is in many traditional societies across Africa.

Boys were usually older than the girls when they got married. Boys got married when they were 18 – 20 years old; girls between 14 and 16.

Normally, girls from richer families got married later than girls from poorer families.

Before marriage, a girl was required to spend a month or so in seclusion. During this period, she would be well-fed – sometimes overfed and fattened – and taught how to be a good wife.

Divorce was also common among the Bakiga. It was common to ask for divorce if one's wife did not bear children. It was also common for women to ask for divorce if the husband was lazy.

Misunderstandings between husbands and wives could also lead to divorce.

Divorced women could remarry but would fetch less bride wealth because they were no longer virgin.

Many matrimonial disputes were settled by elders to save marriages and avoid divorce. And the guilty spouse was normally fined by the elders.

Traditional religion is still strong among the Bakiga although many of them have been converted to Christianity. There are only a few Muslims.

But even some Christians uphold traditional beliefs and subscribe to the tenets of ancestor "worship" –

reverence for their wisdom and guidance from the world beyond and for the role they play in interceding with the Almighty on behalf of the living.

The Bakiga traditionally believe in the existence of a Supreme Being whom they call Ruhanga as the Creator of all things earthly and heavenly; a concept no different from Christianity and which pre-dates the introduction of Christianity to the Bakiga by European missionaries.

But for centuries, they also believed in the cult of Nyabingi. Sacrifices and offerings – including roasted meat and beer – were made to Nyabingi, the spirit of a much-respected rain maker. And they're still made by some people even today because of their strong belief in traditional religion.

The economy of the Bakiga is based on agriculture. They grow mainly sorghum, millet, beans and peas. They also own cows, sheep and goats.

They traditionally also have had excellent iron-smiths making hoes, knives, spears and other implements. They also make excellent pottery, baskets, mats, furniture items and others. They're also very good bee keepers and collect honey.

The Bakiga also have a strong sense of community:

"(Traditionally), the Bakiga lived and worked communally. Most economic activities were done on a communal basis. Grazing, bush clearing, cultivation and harvesting were done communally.

The men cleared the bush while the women tilled the land.

Men worked together to erect round, grass-thatched huts for shelter.

They practiced barter trade amongst themselves and between their neighbors.

The stable foods of Bakiga were sorghum, beans and peas. They supplemented them with pumpkins, yams, meat and a variety of green vegetables. Sufficient food

126

was prepared so that everyone could eat his fill.

It was considered good manners to join in whenever one found given at a meal. One would just wash one's hands and join the others without waiting to be invited.

If a man had more than one wife, all his women had to serve him at each meal.

He could eat the most delicious share of the food among the lot, or all of it if he so wished.

The Bakiga made-beer, *omuramba*, played a significant social role. It had a food component and was an alcoholic drink necessary for social gatherings. *Omuramba* was normally taken from a pot placed in a convenient place.

The men would sit on wooden stools surrounding it and, by means of long tubes, they would drink as they discussed matters affecting their country. The elders would also settle disputes, recite their heroic deeds and their history, and sing and dance around a pot of *omuramba*.

The Bakiga were and still are very good zither (*enanga*) players. They played it alone or in groups.

Utensils

The Bakiga's domestic utensils included baskets, pots, winowing trays, stools, grinding stones, wooden pestles, mortars and mingling ladles.

The other household items were drums and harps for entertainment; spears, bows and arrows for defence and hunting; grass-mats (*ebirago*) for sleeping on and *emishambi* for sitting on.

Political setup

The Bakiga were a segmentary society. Political authority rested in the hands of lineage leaders, *Abakuru b'emiryango*, many of whom had excellent oratory as well as military skills.

They were supposed to be impartial in administering justice.

Some leaders such as *Basubi* emerged to prominence because they had mystical skills. They were rain makers. Others were *Baigirwa,* the mediums of *Nyabingi* cult.

The Bakiga were warlike. They resisted the Batutsi and Bahima incursions. As a politically segmented society, they did not have a standing army. However, they had warlords who would mobilise and lead the people to war in the event of invasion

The warlords were men who had killed a large number of enemies in wars without losing any of their men or weapons. Every able-bodied male was culturally obliged to be a soldier.

Judicial systems

The Bakiga abhorred anti-social activities and if anyone was caught, he was heavily punished. Such activities included stealing, blocking paths, murder, sorcery and night dancing.

In the case of murder for example, the murderer was buried alive in the same grave with the victim.

Virginity was highly esteemed and it was a very serious offence for a girl to get pregnant before marriage." - ("The Bakiga Culture, Origin, Social Setup, Marriage, Political Setup").

The Bakiga are some of the most tradition-bound people in the Great lakes region. And they're deeply rooted in their homeland which is a mountainous area. In fact, the name of their ethnic group, Abakiga (shortened to Bakiga), means "people of the mountains" or "highlanders."

But in spite of the pride they have as a people with their own identity, there's a tendency among a large number of them to adopt Western ways.

They're mesmerised by things Western, and by Western

civilisation which they perceive to be the highest form of human achievement, a phenomenon common in many other parts of Africa.

It's also common in other parts of the Third World because, frankly speaking, of European achievements especially in terms of material civilisation.

But it's a destructive tendency. Modernisation is good but not to the detriment of one's identity and culture. As one member of the Bakiga ethnic group, Festo Karwemera, a respected elder from Kabale, states:

"Accepting the culture of the West is a result of the inferiority complex due to ignorance emanating from the fact that they are the ones introducing civilisation in this land and we tend to assume that everything they do is the best. Their way of living is clean and attractive hence positive because nobody takes trouble to find out how best we can modernise our culture in our own way."

On the other side of Uganda are another Bantu group, the Bagisu, one of the most well-known ethnic groups in the country and in the Great Lakes region.

The Bagisu live mainly in Mbale District on the slopes of Mount Elgon in eastern Uganda. They're a sub-group of the Bamasaaba people of eastern Uganda and are closely related to the Bukusu which is a sub-group the Luhya of Kenya.

The term Bamasaaba is used interchangeably with the term Bagisu, now and then, in spite of the fact that they're different. The Bagisu are Bamasaaba but not all Bamasaaba are Bagisu.

They speak a dialect of the Masaaba language called Lugisu which is not much different from the other dialects within the Bamasaaba group of languages. Lugisu is also understood by the Bukusu.

All the Masaaba understand each other even when they speak different dialects of the Masaaba language. And

Lugisu is also called Lumasaaba. The Bagisu themselves are also known as Bamasaaba.

The Bagisu mainly inhabit the western and southern halves Mountain Elgon. The eastern part of Mount Elgon is in Kenya.

They grow millet, bananas an maize on the well-watered slopes of the mountain mainly for their own consumption. They also grow coffee and cotton as cash crops.

Other crops they grow include sweet and white potatoes, cabbage and other vegctables as well as onions and tomatoes. They also own cattle and other livestock.

Bugisu, their homeland, has the highest population density in Uganda. Almost all land is used for growing crops. Shortage of land has forced many people to leave their traditional homeland and settle elsewhere in Uganda. It also has led to social conflicts now and then through the years.

The Bagisu were introduced to cash crop farming on a significant scale when arabica coffee was brought to them in 1912. The expansion of British colonial rule into Bugisu also played a major role in introducing the Bagisu to a cash economy.

And the people became very successful in the production of cash crops. The climate was highly conducive to farming and the Bagisu were able to produce large amounts of coffee. They also used this as a bargaining tool with the colonial government to extract concessions favourable to them by threatening to withhold production until their demands were met.

The farmers formed the Bugisu Cooperative Union to protect the interests of coffee growers and it became one of the most powerful and most active agricultural cooperative unions in the entire country.

Their economic clout became even more potent because the coffee they grew on the fertile slopes of Mount Elgon was of the highest quality in Uganda. And the total output from that small region constituted more than 10 per cent of the nation's total production.

This provided the Bagisu with a very effective bargaining tool, enabling them to have leverage in their negotiations with the authorities for higher prices for their crops and on other matters pertaining to their interests and well-being.

Land pressure during the early decades of colonial rule forced the Bagisu to migrate northwards, a migratory trend which brought them into conflict with the Sebei who have fought against Gisu dominance for over a century. They saw the Bagisu as invaders encroaching on their territory. And they were not alone in taking that position. Other people felt the same way.

Members of other ethnic groups, the Bagwere and the Bakedi in areas south of Bugisu have also claimed distinct cultural identities and have sought political autonomy.

The Bagisu have no tradition of an early migration from somewhere. And very little is known about their history apart from the fact they're related to a sub-group of the Luhya.

The Luhya are the second largest ethnic in Kenya next to the Kikuyu after surpassing the Luo who once were the second-largest. And because their history is known, it must be inextricably linked with the history of the Bagisu in some ways since the Bukusu who are an integral part of the Luo are related to the Bagisu.

Although not much of their history is known, the Bagisu are believed to have separated from the Bukusu sometime during the 1800s, despite their claim that they have lived where they are all the time; no people have. We all came from somewhere.

The earliest immigrants into Bugisu area are believed to have moved into the Mt. Elgon area during the 16th century from the eastern plains.

Their earliest home is said to have been in the Uasin Gishu plateau of Kenya.

They seem to have been an end product of the mixing of peoples of different origins and cultures, but since their language is Bantu, their predecessors must have been Bantu speakers as well.

Traditionally, the Bagisu had a loose political structure based on clans. Every clan had an elder known as *Umwami we sikoka* which means chief of the clan.

Clan leaders were chosen on the basis of age and wealth. They were responsible for maintaining law and order, and unity as well as continuity of the clan.

They were also responsible for keeping and maintaining the cultural values of the clan and for making sacrifices to the ancestral spirits.

Often, stronger chiefs would extend their influence to other clans but no chief managed to subdue other clans and impose his rule on them, let alone unite them as a single political entity.

Other important figures in the Bugisu traditional society included the rainmakers and the sorcerers.

The Bagisu practise male circumcision although they don't know how and when it became an integral part of their culture. They may have learnt it from the Kalenjin of Kenya.

The men are not considered to be fully grown or mature unless they're circumcised. They take it so seriously that some people are forcibly circumcised as the following case shows.

A man was grabbed in broad daylight by a group of youths in front of cameras and bundled up into a car to face the knife in his lower parts.

He was an elderly man and the youths who grabbed him didn't care about that. They grabbed his arms and legs and had him dangling or hanging like a hammock, his red necktie partly wrapped around his right arm pit. According to a report in the *New Vision*, "Bagisu Youth Grab UPC Man for Circumcision":

"Traffic on Nasser and Nkrumah roads came to a stand-still when an elderly UPC (Uganda People's Congress) veteran from Mbale, Stephen Mujoroto, was 'arrested' by five youth for allegedly dodging *imbalu* (the Bagisu cultural circumcision rite).

Mujoroto, who is a staunch UPC supporter and former Nsangi sub-county chief in the Obote Two regime, was seized at the Canaan Restaurant on Uganda House at about 11:00am.

Well-built youth, one of them believed to be Mujoroto's son, held him by the trousers when they identified him chatting away with colleagues.

Sensing danger, the group fled, thinking the Kampala City law enforcers were arresting criminals.

But after the youth explained their mission, Mujoroto's colleagues allowed them to take him to sort out the 'tribal affair.'

Mujoroto's pretence to be weak and unable to walk did not save him. The youth lifted him into a special hire taxi and took him to Nsambya to face the circumcision knife.

His friends at the scene later said the group had been hunting for Mujoroto the previous day, but on a tip-off, he hid for the whole day.

A youth said to be his son argued that problems had afflicted their family, he blamed on their father's refusal to be circumcised.

He said they had sent several emissaries, including his elder sisters, to persuade him to circumcise to no avail.

The helpless Mujoroto opted to dodge photographers. Most of his friends had known him to be a Muganda. After his arrest, a crowd that gathered blamed Mujoroto for having sex for such a long time without being circumcised." - (Ronnie Kijjambu, "Bagisu Youth Grab UPC Man for Circumcision," *New Vision*, Kampala, Uganda, 25 June 2008).

Even many of those who undergo circumcision have

been converted to Christianity and don't necessarily follow traditional religion. But traditional beliefs including customs such as circumcision are deeply rooted among the Bagisu in general despite widespread influences of modernisation and Western civilisation which have had quite an impact on the traditional way of life.

Many Bagisus, probably the majority, are Christian. There are also some Muslims. But traditional religion is still strong even among a significant number of those who are Christian.

The Ugandan government and aid agencies including UNICEF have accepted the fact that circumcision is a way of life among the Bagisu. And they have made an effort to help the Bagisu make it safer:

"The United Nations Children Fund (UNICEF) has initiated a programme to assist the Bamasaba (Bagisu) in Mbale and Sironko districts modernise circumcision.

President Yoweri Museveni recently told the youths from eastern uganda gathered in Mbale that the Bamasaba ought to modernise the way they handle circumcision to prevent the spread of HIV/AIDS.

Museveni said the use of unsterilised knives on two or more boys would spread the pandemic among Bamasaba.

Bubulo East MP George William Wopuwa, however, said in a statement on Saturday that UNICEF had since 1995 developed a programme to help overcome the problem.

Wopuwa, the former Mbale chief administrative officer, said parents and LCs had under the UNICEF programme been sensitised on the dangers of sharing circumcision knives.

He said traditional surgeons had been trained and certified before being allowed to practice, and that uncircumcised medical doctors had been discouraged from handling the ritual.

Wopuwa said when Museveni came to address the

youths, local leaders including himself and the Eastern youth MP, Wilfred Kajeke, were not invited.

He said if their presence after entry been recognised, they would have answered Museveni. - (Geresom Musamali, "UNICEF to Modernise Bagisu Circumcision," *New Vision*, Kampala, Uganda, 21 October 2003).

One of the most prominent features which distinguishes traditional African societies is adherence to customs and traditions. And the Bagisu are a typical example of that.

Circumcision as a rite of passage is just one of those practices in a panoply of customs and traditions which define many traditional societies in Uganda and other parts of Africa. As Ugandan Professor Kefa M. Otiso of Bowling Green State University in Bowling Green, Ohio, in the United States, states in his book *Culture and Customs in Uganda*:

"Initiation ceremonies were a central feature of traditional Ugandan societies and are to some degree still important even now.

Whereas these ceremonies varied from community to community, they marked the passage from childhood to adulthood or entry into certain social, family, or spiritual groups.

Examples include the outdated tradition of Karimojong boys single-handedly killing a lion or an elephant to prove their manhood and readiness for marriage; the circumcision of boys – and in some cases girls – to mark the transition from childhood to adulthood among the Bakonjo and Bamba, Bagisu, Sabiny (sic) (Sabine), and Sebei; blood brotherhood ceremonies amon the Batoore and Banyankore that united two unrelated people into bonds, obliging them to relate and support each other as biological brothers; and *Mukeli Gagi*, ritual marriages that initiate some Alur women's husbands into certain

135

spiritual/religious cults.

All these initiation ceremonies usually included training in the rights and responsibilities of the initiates.

Uganda's rapid cultural change as a result of modernization is either undermining or transforming many of these traditional initiation ceremonies. For instance, the role of circumcision as a rite of passage from childhood to adulthood among the Bakonjo and Bamba, Bagisu, Sabiny (Sabine), and Sebei is being transformed, and, in some cases, is being displaced by passage through the formal school system....

The Bagisu, have, perhaps, the most elaborate boy initiation practices in Uganda....The origin of Bagisu circumcision is unclear. But there are several competing explanations, one of which is that it improves a man's sexual prowess. The Bagisu circumcise 12- to 15-year-old boys once every two years." - (Kefa M. Otiso, *Culture and Customs of Uganda*, Westport, Connecticut, USA, Greenwood Press, 2006, p. 103).

Although the Bagisu are Bantu and practise cicumcision, it's important to note that circumcision is not as widespread among the Bantu as it is among Nilotics. Almost all Nilotic groups such as the Karamojong, the Kalenjin, the Maasai and others practise circumcision.

That's not the case among many Bantu groups in different parts of East Africa including neighbouring Tanzania. For example, the Nyakyusa and the Ndali of southwestern Tanzania don't have their men – or their women – circumcised.

But in societies where it's practised, even those who may be against it succumb to the knife because there's so much social pressure exerted on them. Failure to do so leads to ostracisation.

Not only do they become social outcasts; they're not considered manly and may not even be able to marry, something which is frowned upon in most traditional

136

societies across Africa.

Among Bantu groups which don't traditionally practise circumcision, the only people who must be circumcised are Muslims since that's mandatory according to Islam.

But it's also a very painful experience. And some people who have come under the knife have written about their ordeal, as did, for example, Nelson Mandela, a Xhosa, in his book *Long Walk to Freedom*.

The Xhosa, the second-largest ethnic group in South Africa after the Zulu, are among the Bantu groups which practise circumcision.

Among the Bagisu, there's also acceptance of both – the pain and the necessity to be circumcised – and also of the pride in their culture which holds the people together as a group with their own unique identity and way of life. And it's a wonderful journey into manhood, however painful. As Aboubakar Famau stated in his report in *The East African Tribune*, appropriately entitled, "Bagisu Circumcision, a Painful Life Time Journey into Manhood":

"Circumcision in the **Bagisu** community is such an important occasion and as a result, the ceremony normally attracts a huge number of people from different walks of life.

Among the attendants are diplomats, religious leaders, members of parliaments, tourists and other well wishers.

Thousands of cheerful well-wishers would gather as early as dawn at a place called **Bumutoto** to mark the official opening of the **Imbalu** circumcision ceremony. **Bumutoto** is in the Eastern part of Uganda in Mbale district which is the original home to **Bamasaba** people who are very rich in culture.

The literal meaning of the word **Imbalu** or **Ipalu** is cutting round or trimming of the man's penis. The knives used for this work are sharpened on a special stone and are not supposed to be used for any other work. The job of

137

circumcision is a hereditary responsibility handed down from fathers to sons and this is the only way one can become a circumciser.

The circumcision among the **Bamasaba** takes place every two even years. The well-organized opening ceremony lasts for 24 hours and must take place at the **Bumutoto** cultural site; this is a place where traditionally it is believed to be the original land of the Bagisu ancestors.

The candidates are presented to the audience, dancers decorated with six to eight thigh bells and two hand bells jump high in air to help the initiates on their once in a lifetime chance to make the journey into complete manhood.

The candidates are normally smeared with a mixture of miller and cassava flour. The candidates are lined up for the cutting while a he goat or bull is being slaughtered as a sacrifice in the same courtyard where candidates are to undergo pain. The animal's heart is then stuck on a stick and displayed for everyone to witness. This is a sacrifice to the ancestral spirits called Bamasaba.

The candidates are then made to stand straight and firm on a sack, holding a stick across the shoulders, and very quickly, the foreskin is cut off. The fastest surgeon can finish the operation in less than a minute.

If the candidate has successfully finished the ritual without fear, women will continue dancing, singing and drumming as a way of congratulating the candidates for his endurance and courage. **Kadodi,** a popular traditional dance is normally played; in fact any visitor will have mixed feelings at the sight of the **kadodi** dance. It is a popular dance in town. Normally it attracts young beautiful ladies who twist their waist up and down while excited men follow on.

The men spend along period of their time in isolation until wounds are healed. The elders then prepare to officially receive the initiates back into the community with elaborate ceremonies so that they can begin a new life of adulthood.

The cowards who fear the knife, and instead choose to disappear into thin air, have to pay the **Gisu** debt.

That is if their fellow **Bagisu** spot them, whenever they are, they will be caught and the circumcision will be organized immediately. Some who have escaped may be later exposed and denounced by their wives. In this affair, **Bagisu** men can only run but can not hide, because wherever they are, they will be caught and returned back for the real circumcision." - (Aboubakar Famau, ""Bagisu Circumcision, a Painful Life Time Journey into Manhood," *The East African Tribune*, 22 March 2007).

Another ethnic group that's examined in this study is the Lugbara of northwestern Uganda.

They're one of the largest Nilotic groups in the country. They live mainly in the West Nile region of Uganda and in the adjoining area of the Democratic Republic of Congo (DRC).

Their language, Lugbara, has many dialects. But the people who speak those dialects understand each other. In addition to the Madi, the Lugbara are also related to the Kakwa and understand each other when they speak their languages.

They're also closely related to the Logo, 'Bale (Lendu), and Keliko, and are distantly related to the Azande and the Mangbetu.

And they and the Madi, their neighbours to the east, are the only representatives of the eastern Sudanic language group in eastern Africa.

Their cultural symbol is the leopard. And they're very conscious of their singular identity geographically, linguistically, and culturally. Their plateau is very distinct from the landscapes of most of their neighbours.

They're farmers and also own livestock, mainly cattle and goats. They also have sheep.

Before the cattle epidemics of the 1980s, they had far greater herds. Cattle, goats, and sheep are also killed for ancestral sacrifices and meat is consumed by those attending the ceremonies. The Lugbara also sell hides and skins, earning valuable income.

They also own poultry and are known in Uganda as the main keepers of the guineafowl which is known as *ope* in their language.

There's also a sharp division of labour between men and women. Men clear the fields while the women do the rest of the work. Men also hunt and herd cattle while women do domestic work.

The Lugbara irrigate their farms. And some of their fields are also under permanent or shifting cultivation..

Traditionally, their social organisation was based on clans and sub-clans. Chiefdoms came later, introduced by the colonial rulers who appointed locally influential men as chiefs. Below the chefs were headmen The Lugbara never had a king or paramount ruler.

The chiefs usually formed alliances to ensure security and mobilise forces against attacks by other ethnic groups. But they did not have a standing army.

Every able-bodied man was duty-bound to protect his village. Therefore all men were automatically considered to be soldiers ready to answer the call whenever needed. However, military service was never considered to be a permanent duty.

Men hold formal authority over their kin but older women informally exercise considerable domestic and lineage authority. Land is traditionally not sold or rented; it's held by lineages. Women are also allocated rights of use by their husbands' lineage elders.

Marriage is forbidden between members of the same clan or with a man's or woman's mother's close kin. And polygamy is widespread. About a third of the men have more than one wife. However, most secondary wives are those inherited from their brothers or fathers' brothers. A number of other African tribes have the same custom of inheriting wives from dead brothers.

Some even inherit wives of their dead fathers in a number of traditional societies on the continent. Their step mothers become their wives, although this is not practised by the Lugbara.

Divorce is relatively unusual among the Lugbara. And only men can seek divorce. The parents or relatives of the divorced woman or women are required to return cattle given to them as dowry. But if there are children involved, a different formula is used. For every child born, a cow is kept, not returned.

The main grounds for divorce are adultery and barrenness. In fact, in many traditional societies in Africa, a man can ask for divorce if a woman can not bear children.

There are no forms of initiation at puberty, but children of about 6 undergo forehead cicatrization and excision of the lower four incisors.

The Lugbara country is open, composed of countless small ridges with streams between them. The compounds and fields are set on the ridges. Houses are round. They're made of mud and wattle and thatch.

If a man has more than one wife, he moves from one house to another in turn. The house, and especially its hearth, is very much a female domain.

Traditional religion has played a prominent in the lives of the Lugbara. And it continues to do so.

Even before the coming of Europeans who introduced Christianity, the Lugbra believed in a single deity called *Adroa*. They believed, as they still do today, that He created the world and everything in it.

They also believe that there's a world of spirits and departed ancestors. The spirits influence the affairs of men, as do departed ancestors, and sacrifices must be offered to appease them.

The Lugbara believe that the living interact with the

dead of the same lineage and that this relationship is permanent. Because of this close relationship, the dead know what's going on among the living whom they still consider to be their children.

However, in some circumstances, the dead send sickness to the living, in order to remind them that they are acting custodians of the Lugbara lineages and their shrines.

Also, there have been prophets among the Lugbara during hard times and periods of crisis. Divinely-inspired messages, according to those who believe this, have involved the reorganisation of the social order, among other things.

The most famous prophet among the Lugbara was Rembe who led an anti-European healing cult in 1916. He was actually a member of the Kakwa tribe and lived about 40 miles north of Lugbara.

But many of them have also embraced Christianity and are mostly Catholic.

There are also a few Muslims in the region, especially in the few small townships. These are usually Nubians – also called Nubi – and they are not typical Lugbara.

The most prominent Muslim from the West Nile region was Idi Amin who came from the neighbouring Kakwa tribe.

Although the Lugbara are engaged in agriculture, they're not commercial farmers.

Cash crops were encouraged during the colonial period, but, owing to edaphic and climatic factors and the long distance to the nearest markets for cash crops, few have been profitable.

The best markets are in the southern part of the country where the capital Kampala is also located. That's hundreds of miles away, discouraging many people in the West Nile from engaging in commercial agriculture.

Groundnuts, sunflower, cotton, and tobacco have all been tried as commercial crops. But only the latter two, cotton and tobacco, have had some success.

The main export has been that of male labour to the Indian-owned sugar plantations and the African-owned farms of southern Uganda. About one-quarter of the men are absent at any one time, making the Lugbara some of the most well-known migrant workers in Uganda.

Almost all farming is restricted to the subsistence level. They grow a variety of crops but cassava is now their staple food. Traditionally, they have relied on millet and sorghum.

Besides millet and sorghum, they also grow pigeon peas and a variety of root crops including sweet potatoes. But with their increasing dependency on cassava, their diet has deteriorated. Traditionally, they had a highly nutritious diet.

They also grow maize for local consumption and for making local beer. Their main cash crop is tobacco.

Their land is very fertile. They are also known to be very good farmers even though they grow crops on a small scale mainly for their own consumption.

They are, in general tall people, taller than the average Ugandan, and are skillful hunters using mainly bows and long arrows.

They're also known for making very good baskets and pots. Besides pottery and basketry, they have few other aesthetic products. They don't make elaborate carvings or skillfully handle metal.

The iron-smiths among them are members of an ethnic group called Ndu. These skilled workers make iron tools and weapons. They live scattered among the Lugbara settlements and are held in awe by them. They're also feared by the Lugbara as if they have some mystical powers because of their iron-working skills.

But the Lugbara also have a reputation as fierce fighters and very defensive of their land. It was this ability to fight and defend themselves which saved them from being enslaved by the marauding Arab slave traders who were active to the north and west during the 19th century.

Although many of them have been converted to Christianity, modernisation has not penetrated their society as much as it has other parts of Uganda especially in the southern kingdoms. Theirs is a much more traditional way of life, and conservative.

There have been complaints that after the country won independence, the Lugbara were ignored by the government of Milton Obote.

The situation changed when Idi Amin seized power. The Lugbara got many favours from him during his tenure mainly because he himself came from the West Nile region and saw the Lugbara as his people who were also related to his tribe, the Kakwa.

When Obote regained power in 1980, the Lugbara were subjected to brutal treatment by government soldiers who were fighting insurgents in the West Nile and other parts of Uganda trying to overthrow Obote.

In fact, one of the strongest opposition strongholds was in the West Nile region where remnants of Idi Amin's army had settled. They were resolutely opposed to Obote's rule, and many local people suffered as a result.

Some people claimed the Lugbara and other people in the West Nile region were subjected to brutal near-genocide by Obote's second regime.

But they also inflicted a lot damage on the country when they, together with the Kakwa, constituted a disproportionately large number of soldiers in the Ugandan army under Idi Amin after Amin eliminated the Langi and the Acholi who once dominated the army during Obote's tenure.

Amin recruited them as his fellow tribesmen to consolidate his position and to provide a counterweight against his opponents. In fact, he was a product of both tribes although he was identified as a Kakwa. His father was a Kakwa and his mother a Lugbara, with his ethnicity determined by patrilineal descent as is the case in many

144

African societies.

His reliance on the people from the West Nile, his home region, to back up his regime and stay in power is a common feature of African politics and leadership dominated by tribal and regional loyalties.

Besides the Kakwa and the Lugbara, other people from the West Nile who were recruited into the army by Amin were the Madi, the Alur and the Nubians who were of Sudanese descent but who had settled in the West Nile region. He even recruited some who were Sudanese.

In fact, both the Kakwa and the Nubians live in West Nile and in Sudan, with the Kakwa straddling the Ugandan-Congolese-Sudanese border.

The regional loyalties were also fuelled by the rivalry between Amin and Obote. Although both northerners, they came from different parts of the north. And according to an analysis provided by three Ugandan scholars in their book *The Social Origins of Violence in Uganda, 1964 – 1985*:

"Like Obote, Amin consolidated his base in the army by using his own ethnic groups. While the friendship between Amin and Obote lasted, their Lwo and Sudanic recruits cooperated to provide a strong military base for both men.

After the *coup d'etat* Amin brutally eliminated most of the Lwo (Luo) speakers, especially the Langi and Acholi.

In March 1971 more than thirty Acholi/Langi soldiers were dynamited at Makindye Barracks. On 22 July 1971 about 150 to 500 Acholis and Langis from Simba Battalion, Mbarara, were herded into trucks, taken to an isolated ranch, and gunned down.

On going to Israel and Europe in July 1971, Amin gave orders for the elimination of the Langi and Acholi soldiers, fearing they might organize a *coup*. At Mbarara, soldiers from these ethnic groups were separated from the rest and taken to their deaths.

145

On 9 July 1971 about twenty new Acholi/Langi recruits were killed; more died the following day. Between 10 and 14 July 1971 some fifty Acholi/Langi soldiers were killed at Magamaga Ordnance Depot.

Further massacres of these ethnic groups occurred at military barracks at Masindi, Soroti, and Kitgum. On a February 1972, about 117 soldiers and other security men of the Obote regime were mowed down as they tried to escape.

What is upsetting about Ugandans is that while the Langi and Acholi suffered, many laughed, thinking their own turn would never come, just as they had laughed at the Baganda in 1966.

But wherever violence occurs in the state, it eventually overflows to everyone. By 1971 the fires of political violence that had been lit at Nakulabye were spreading into the rural areas of Apaci, Lira, and Gulu. Soon, they would scorch all the land.

Amin based his support in the army on the Kakwa and Nubi, with the former Anyanya Zairous and Sudanese forming the nucleus to which were attached other West Nile groups like the Madi, the Lugbara, and the Alur." - (Abdu Basajabaka Kawalya Kasozi, Nakanyike Musisi, James Mukooza Sejjengo, *The Social Origins of Violence in Uganda, 1964 – 1985*, Montreal, Canada, McGill-Queen's University Press, 1994, p. 111).

But the ethnic alliance of the West Nile groups under Amin's regime did not last long because of Amin himself. He turned against some groups, and thus helped to weaken and undermine his own regime.

Yet, in spite of all that, members of the alienated groups did not conspire against Amin. They feared that once he was gone, they would also be hunted down because they had been closely associated with him and had even worked for him, wreaking havoc across the country at the behest of their boss.

And in many cases, they did that of their volition since they saw themselves as wielders of power inextricably linked with their kinsman at the top who was the military head of state.

But it was Amin himself who engineered his own downfall, first by weakening his base in the army:

"His political fortunes began to decline when he narrowed his base by gradually trimming the large West Nile support in the army.

From 1971 to 1972 the Alur were gradually marginalized. Lieutenant-Colonel Ochima, an Alur with a following in the army, was imprisoned in July 1971 and shot the following year.

After the 1972 invasion of Uganda by Ugandan exiles (based in Tanzania), Alurs were removed from most strategic positions.

The turn of the Madi came in late 1972. Amin accused all Madi of drunkenness and removed and removed them from sensitive positions. He then called in Madi elders to explain to them the crimes of 'their sons.'

Pruning of the Lugbara began in early 1972. Their 'son,' Obitre-Gama, was dismissed in March as minister of Internal Affairs, brought back in a minor portfolio, and again dismissed in mid-1973.

Another Lugbara, Lieutenant-Colonel Ondoga, the ambassador to Moscow, was recalled and made minister of Foreign Affairs. He was later publicly dismissed and his body was found floating in a river.

Many Lugbaras were killed at this time.

Amin dismissed his Lugbara wife, though he took the opportunity to divorce two more from other ethnic groups as a show of 'tribal impartiality.'

By 1975 the Kakwa-Nubi-Anyanya core had closed ranks and was the foundation of Amin's power machine. They held most of the strategic positions, manned key installations, and easily grouped whenever there was

147

trouble.

The other alienated West Nile groups did not fight Amin because they rightly judged that it was not in their interest to overthrow him. If he were overthrown, they would be punished for their natural association with him....

Subsequent events proved them right: the Acholi/Langi militia brutalized the whole population of West Nile in 1980 – 83 for being associated with Amin on ethnic basis." - (Ibid., pp. 111 – 112).

That was during Obote's second regime after he returned to power in 1980. It was during that period that some critics of Obote claimed the killings in West Nile by his army amounted to near-genocide.

Even during his years in power before he was overthrown by Amin, he was not very comfortable with him. But he could not do anything about it because he feared that he would alienate Amin's supporters in the army even though the majority of the soldiers were Acholi and Langi who supported him, not Amin. As E.D. Mwamula-Lubandi states in his book *Clan Theory in African Development Studies Analysis: Reconsidering African Development Promotive Bases*:

"Obote put Amin under house arrest in 1969. He was scared to kill him or do something serious since this would have annoyed Lugbara, Kakwa and Nubian forces." - (E.D. Mwamula-Lubandi, *Clan Theory in African Development Studies Analysis: Reconsidering African Development Promotive Bases*, University Press of America, original from the University of Michigan, 1992, p. 189).

During the first regime of Obote after the country won independence from Britain, the Lugbara and other people of the West Nile were largely ignored in terms of political

148

representation at high levels in the government.

They were virtually marginalised and did not play a major role in the political developments which took place in Uganda after independence.

But after Amin seized power from Obote in January 1971, many people from the West Nile – especially the Kakwa, the Lugbara, the Alur, the Madi and Nubians – became major actors on the nation's political scene mostly as soldiers and as security and intelligence officers protecting Amin. Some of them also held high government positions including cabinet and ambassadorial posts among many others.

The tragedy is that all those alliances – under both Obote and Amin – were marriages of convenience without solid foundation. They also were not in the best interest of the nation which was still struggling to transcend ethnic and regional loyalties in order to create a truly national identity embracing all Ugandans. Instead, ethnicity became paramount, fuelling challenges against the legitimacy of the state as an institution of authority over the whole country.

Many Ugandans did not accept that back then, and they still don't today. Their ethno-regional loyalties and interests, hence ethnicity and regionalism, come first at the expense of national unity and identity.

While I have not written about every ethnic group in Uganda – besides briefly mentioning most of them here and there – I have focused on a number of them to provide regional balance.

In fact, I have covered all the major ones in detail. Uganda has 25 indigenous tribes or ethnic groups. It does not have very many ethnic groups like neighbouring Tanzania which has 126, and Kenya which has 42.

The ones I have looked at here, in detail, in the Ugandan context also constitute families of ethnic groups or are representative of ethnic clusters – Bantu and Nilotic – in different parts of the country.

But the survey can not be complete without including the Batwa who are neither Bantu nor Nilotic.

The Batwa, or Twa, live in southwestern Uganda. They're also known as Pygmies.

They're also found across the border in neighbouring Congo and Rwanda.

They live in the forest and have a strong attachment to their homeland. They believe that when God made them, He wanted them to live in the forest and protect it.

They also like to be close to nature in an environment where it's quiet and peaceful. And they may the original people together with the so-called Bushmen.

They have lived in the forest for a long time. This has enabled them to develop survival skills unmatched by members of other ethnic groups who may try to live in this kind of environment.

The forest provides them with herbs for medicine. They use traditional medicine for all kinds of ailments and don't depend on modern medicine for treatment.

They're also excellent hunters. They use bows and arrows, spears and machetes as well as knives. Their reputation as excellent users of bows and arrows is legendary. They also use the same weapons to defend themselves.

One of the biggest items in their diet is honey which is also excellent for fighting diseases. And besides meat, wild fruit as well as vegetables and mushrooms are an integral part of their diet.

They have been mostly hunter-gatherers, some in the mountainous forests, and some in forest savannah or lake environments.

They're despised by their neighbours but maintain their dignity by living in isolation.

Many of their neighbours don't even see them as human.

Their neighbours are mostly Bantu except the Tutsi. They're also known as forest people who live in the rainforests of east-central Africa and as far afield as Cameroon and the Central African Republic.

Other countries in which they live are the Democratic Republic of Congo, Rwanda, Burundi, Congo-Brazzaville and Gabon.

But their means of livelihood have been severely affected through the years, reducing them to desperate conditions in some parts of the east-central and west-central regions of Africa.

In all those countries, they suffer discrimination, only in varying degrees. And their plight can be better understood when look at in a larger context embracing all these groups of marginalised people in that part of the continent:

"The Batwa of south west Uganda number only a few thousand people and are one of the hunter-gatherer and ex-hunter-gatherer peoples collectively known as the forest peoples (or 'Pygmies') of the Central African rainforests.

The situation of the different forest peoples who live throughout Central Africa varies tremendously, and they probably collectively number between 250,000 and 300,000 people.

Forest peoples tend to suffer severe discrimination at the hands of their farming neighbours and others; but they also to a greater or lesser extent, manage to maintain a resilient egalitarian social system.

Severe discrimination is most evident for those groups, such as the Batwa of south west Uganda, who no longer have access to their forest resource base, but it is also a powerful enduring theme, and often a dominant one, for forest-based groups in relationship to neighbouring farmers.

The three largest groups of forest peoples who still, to a great extent, retain their forest resource base are: the Mbuti (and Efe) of the Ituri Forest in the Democratic Republic of Congo, the Baka of south eastern Cameroon

151

and north western Congo Brazzaville, and the Aka (and Mbendjelle) of northern Congo-Brazzaville and the Central African Republic.

For many of these groups the forest continues to provide them with an independent resource base, and it also provides the context for the beliefs and experiences which underpin an economy of sharing and a political system which is essentially fluid and egalitarian.

In these contexts, forest peoples are, to varying degrees, able to exert some or great autonomy in determining the nature of their interaction with their farming neighbours and with the more recent incomers to the forest.

The recent political upheavals and civil war in the region has had an especially severe impact on the Batwa of Rwanda, Burundi, and eastern DR Congo; and has accelerated the ongoing marginalisation of these groups who are mostly former rather than present-day hunter-gatherers.

The ongoing logging in south west Cameroon and the construction of the Chad-Cameroon oil pipeline may have a similarly devastating impact on the Bakola there.

For many of the Batwa of Uganda, Rwanda, Burundi and DR Congo, their resource base has either been destroyed or denied them, through deforestation, through the control exerted over them by neighbouring farmers, or more recently through conservation projects restricting or denying their access to the forest. As a result, groups such as the Batwa of south west Uganda have been reduced to virtual serfdom and poverty....

Central African governments tend to see such Forest Peoples as needing to be sedentarised – both for tax and control purposes, and in order to ensure that the rest of the country is not stigmatised as backward by association with such people....

(Bantu and other) farmers have historically had an ambivalent attitude towards these hunter-gatherers:

sometimes viewing them as slaves and barely human, and sometimes as equals or even as the original civilising beings.

Where, in the past, these hunter-gatherers have been crucial to farmers, enabling them to benefit from forest produce, protecting them from forest spirits, and ritually ensuring the fertility of their fields, today in many parts of Central Africa, including south west Uganda, the forests have dwindled in importance and as a result hunter-gatherers and ex-hunter-gatherers such as the Batwa have become marginalised and severely discriminated against.

Where their universally acknowledged status as the original inhabitants of the forest and the region once served to underwrite their autonomous forest life and their ability to relate to others as equals, that status is often now seen as a symbol of their backwardness.

Any prior rights to resources which they may have had have been over-ridden, first by colonial and then by national governments who ignore their traditional systems of land ownership." - (Justin Kenrick, Forest Peoples Programme with the United Organisation for Batwa Development in Uganda (UOBDU), "The Batwa of South West Uganda," October 2000. See the recent research into the situation of the Batwa in eastern DRC (Barume & Jackson: 2000), and of the Batwa throughout the Great Lakes region (Lewis: 2000). See also a recent survey of different forest peoples' situations throughout Central Africa (Luling & Kenrick: 1998).

Many Batwas in southwestern Uganda have been forced by the government to move out of the forest, disrupting their traditional way of life and causing extreme hardship for them. They have lost their homes and means of livelihood without getting any help from the government.

In 1991, the Bwindi and Mgahinga National Parks were established in southwestern Uganda, causing great suffering to Batwa and other neighbouring local communities.

The Batwa are by far the most affected group since they no longer have access to their forest resources, and so their forest-based participation in the local economy has been destroyed and they have been reduced to being landless labourers.

Not only did they lose their territorial rights and ancestral forest homes; they were denied human rights:

"In addition to their forced expulsion from the living in or using their forests, the Batwa of Uganda suffer severe discrimination at the hands of other communities.

They experience marginalisation and discrimination, a lack of land, of access to formal education and to employment and even to secure an area to put up temporary dwellings involves having to work long hours in others' fields.

They are not represented – locally or nationally. Instead of being able to base their livelihoods in the forests using their traditional skills, they now depend on labouring – and even begging – to support their livelihoods.

To make matters even worse, there has been very slow movement in terms of achieving some form of compensation for the Batwa for their loss of their territories." - (Penninah Zaninka and Justin Kenrick, "The Batwa Organize to Reassert Their Rights," *World Rainfroest Movement (WRM) Bulletin*, No. 62, September 2002).

But they're survivors. They have lived in the forest for thousands of years. They know how to fend for themselves. Their skills have ensured their survival. But there are those who fear the worst.

The Batwa may be extinct one day. According to a report by the Unrepresented Nations and Peoples Organization (UNPO):

"Hunger could wipe out the Batwa ethnic group in Uganda unless urgent intervention is enforced, researchers have said.

A study conducted by Rose Mwebaza, the coordinator of Uganda Land Alliance for Coalition of Pastoral Civil Society Organizations (COPASCO), reads in part:

'Many Batwa are dying of hunger because they do not know how to survive outside the forest.'

The study, titled 'Lessons from the Batwa Experience in the Conservation and Management of Bwindi Game Park,' states that the loss of access to Bwindi Impenetrable Forest which supported the Batwa subsistence has left them in unfamiliar territory, virtually threatening their survival.

'There are reports that some Batwa go for four to five days without eating and they have resorted to eating banana peels from their Bahutu neighbours. Most young children have run to the urban centres to escape from the hunger and now work as porters and many others have turned to begging for survival,' Mwebaza notes.

She blamed the Ugandan government for gazetting the Bwindi Impenetrable Game Park without consulting the Batwa, the indigenous community in the vicinity.

'It is clear that the government initiated the process of gazetting Bwindi without involving or considering the participation of the Batwa in the process. Most of the planning was done in the capital city, Kampala, hundreds of miles away from Bwindi,' Mwebaza said.

'The Batwa had no knowledge of what was going on and only got to know of the process when Bwindi was already gazetted and they were being asked to vacate the area,' she added.

The game park is a world heritage site located in south-western Uganda. Situated on the edge of the western Rift Valley, the park is 32,092 square kilometres and borders the Democratic Republic of the Congo (DRC).

The Batwa, who inhabit part of south-western Uganda, are part of a group that is also found in the DRC, Rwanda and Burundi. Their population is estimated at 70,000 to 87,000 dispersed over 100,000 square kilometres and make between 0.02% and 0.7% of the total population in the various countries they occupy.

Mwebaza, who is also a lecturer at the Faculty of Law Makerere University, further asserted in her study that as these groups become smaller, their ability to come up with a common stand and demand for participation in the decision making process reduces. She noted that this has resulted in the complete expropriation of their land and source of livelihood.

'As scarcity and the fight for survival intensify among the Batwa, they are breaking up into even smaller groups and sometimes as individuals to try and find a way to continue existing. In addition, the Batwa have slowly lost their identity, which has over the decades been built on Bwindi and their ability to survive in it,' Mwebaza observed.

She added:

'The Batwa are not only facing a crisis of survival, but also of identity. It is clear that the very existence of the Batwa is under threat. The problem of Batwa identity and survival is made worse by government policies that are now aimed at assimilating the Batwa into the wider community. There is no clear organizational force in Uganda from among the Batwa demanding to retain their way of life or the continued access to their traditional shrines within the Bwindi forest.'

However, against all odds and in spite of their phenomenal marginalisation and the threat of extinction facing them because of loss of their source of livelihood, some Batwa have joined the international indigenous rights movement to reinforce their existence.

'International organizations have taken on the Batwa struggle and have formed a 'Twa Support Group' to ensure effective communication and sharing of information between them and to avoid duplicating activities. The Batwa, with the support of international organizations, have embarked on a process that will enable them to represent themselves effectively at local, national and international levels,' Mwebaza said.

But despite those efforts illiteracy has blocked the Batwa from articulating their plight in the necessary for a, resulting in their fate being overlooked.

'Batwa are illiterate and so they not only fail to keep up with proposed government changes that affect them but they also cannot effectively participate even when they are aware of the up-coming changes,' Mwebaza further indicated.

'In a meeting with local and international NGO's working to support the Batwa in Uganda, the chairman of the Batwa in Uganda informed the group that there are only six educated Batwa in Uganda and even then, they are in secondary school and so they cannot be involved in the decision making process.'" - (Unrepresented Nations and Peoples Organization, "Batwa Ethnic Group Faces Extinction," 9 August 2006).

While some observers don't go to that extreme, saying the Batwa face extinction, many of them are equally apprehensive of the situation and concede that if nothing is done to protect them, they face a bleak future.

The Ugandan government and others in the region – as well as the ones in southern Africa especially Botswana where another marginalised people, the San and the Khoi live – are pursuing a policy of modernisation to force these people to abandon their traditional way of life and become part of the modern society.

But such a policy is bound to fail because the people who are being forced to change don't want to change. And even for those who want to do so, more often than not, only grudgingly, it's obvious that they can not change right away because adaptation can not be done overnight.

Tragically, in this clash of civilisations or cultures, the marginalised groups end up being the losers. It's also a form of cultural genocide.

And their future is indeed bleak. According to a report by Thomas Fessy, BBC World Service, "Batwa Face Uncertain Future":

"Just after dawn, as the fog slowly leaves the slopes of the Muhabura volcano, some Batwa people make their way to the neighbouring farms hoping to get a job for the day.

The Nyarusisa community is landless. Families are squatting on other people's land or live in shabby camps with no sanitation.

The Muhabura volcano is one of the three inactive volcanoes that make the south-west Ugandan border with Rwanda and the Democratic Republic of Congo.

Right next to the Mgahinga National Park's boundaries, the slopes of these mountains are intensively cultivated and settled by dominant Bufumbira and Hutu people.

Nearly two decades ago, the Batwa lived in the mountain forest of Mgahinga as well as in the deep forest of Bwindi, called the Impenetrable Forest.

In these two places, where a small area of forest is surrounded by large numbers of poor rural farmers trying to scrape by and live off the land, conservation is a tricky issue.

'It is a question of trying to balance the protection of the forest with the needs of the local communities,' says Alastair McNeilage, from the Wildlife Conservation Society, who works at Bwindi.

When the area was divided into three forest reserves - Mgahinga, Echuya and Bwindi - in the early 1930s, the Batwa stayed where they had been living for generations.

However, when the Ugandan government decided to reinforce the protection of the mountain gorilla habitat, the

Batwa were moved from their lands to make way for national parks.

They have become conservation refugees. Anthropologist Chris Sandbrook explains that in the early days of conservation 'local people were excluded from protected areas and kept out with some kind of law enforcement, which has been called fortress conservation.'

Up on a hill, between the Echuya forest and the Bwindi Park, community leader Sembagare Francis recalls:

'One day, we were in the forest when we saw people coming with machine guns and they told us to get out of the forest. We were very scared so we started to run not knowing where to go and some of us disappeared. They either died or went somewhere we didn't know. As a result of the eviction, everybody is now scattered.'

Conservationists, back then, saw local communities as a major threat to wildlife. John Makombo from the Uganda Wildlife Authority says that they aimed to achieve 'sustainable conservation.'

'Originally, when the Batwa were living in the forest they were hunting down all the fauna and that was eradicating almost all the animals: the gorillas were in danger, the chimps were in danger,' Mr Makombo said.

'So, it was not wise to leave [the Batwa] inside the forest. I think it was better to manage them when they are outside the forest.'

Conservation outcasts

It seems that the Batwa have suffered more than other people from the creation of the parks because they were the people whose livelihoods were most closely related to the forest.

Even now, they tend to be the poorest and most marginalised people who have fewer opportunities to benefit from tourism and other development programmes that have come along with the parks.

They live in unsanitary housing conditions, typically mud huts where the rain comes through.

According to the United Organisation for Batwa Development in Uganda (UOBDU), most are unable to invest in permanent structures as they fear being removed by the owner of the land on which they are squatting.

UOBDU co-ordinator Penninah Zaninka says that the government 'should really think of resettling the Batwa and give them better shelters so that they could benefit from development projects that the government is doing for other citizens of Uganda.'

The government seems to have handed over its responsibility to the few organisations and church groups looking at the plight of the Batwa people.

Minister of State for Tourism Serapio Rukundo told the BBC that it is for 'their future that the government told them to leave the forest.'

He added: 'The question is also: what is the quality of life you would like the Batwa to live? And what rights are you going to guarantee for the animals?'

However, the quality of life of the Batwa does not seem to be taken into account by conservation programmes.

UWA's John Makombo defended their approach: 'Their conditions of living are not our responsibility. Questions of poverty are not our responsibility.'

Eroding culture

Targeted worldwide by the many tribes evicted from protected areas, big conservation NGOs have now made it clear that they do not support the creation of protected areas that displace indigenous people.

WWF International director general James Leape says mistakes have been made in the past.

'I think that we have, over the last 20 years, learnt case

160

after case that it's a mistake to see conservation and development as opposed to each other. It's clear that we will only be successful in conservation if it works for local communities.'

Nevertheless, hardly any of the staff working for the parks is from the Batwa communities.

'They don't give us a chance to work for the park, when they select people they forget the Batwa,' a member of the Batwa community said.

The Batwa also complain that they cannot access the forest to practice their traditional culture. Most of them fear the park rangers.

'They told us that if anybody goes in the forest to carry out any activities they would be killed,' says Bernard, an elder.

'We have all our traditional equipment here like things to help us collect honey, bows and arrows for hunting - but we haven't taught our children. Even if we wanted to teach them, we can't in this community as we would need to practice in the forest. I'm really not happy that our children cannot learn our culture.'

While their forest-based culture is eroded, the United Nations passed a declaration at the end of last year on the rights of indigenous peoples. It says they cannot be forcibly removed from their lands or territories.

Margaret Lokawua, board member of the UN Permanent Forum on Indigenous Issues, says the Batwa have a case for compensation but it will take some time.

'The Batwa can use this declaration to defend their case and I think they will win; the government will give them a piece of land," she explained.

'But looking at the governments that we have in Africa, it takes time. Meanwhile the Batwa will continue to be squatters on other people's land.'

There may be some hope, but this declaration is non-binding and Uganda was absent when it was adopted." - (Thomas Fessy, "Batwa Face Uncertain Future," BBC

World Service, 9 March 2008).

The marginalisation of the Batwa may be the most extreme case in Uganda. But there are other groups which don't get as much attention from the government as the big ones do.

And while it's true that Uganda is composed of many ethnic groups, it's equally true that the history of the country has largely been shaped by only a few of them, especially the ones which had powerful kingdoms or other major centres of power.

One of these major traditional centres of power – besides Buganda, Bunyoro, Ankole, Toro and Busoga – is Teso.

The people of this area are called Iteso. They are a branch of the eastern Nilotic language speakers and are one of the largest ethnic groups in Uganda.

The eastern branch of Nilotic is divided into the Teso-speaking and Maa-speaking (Maasai) branches. The Teso branch is further divided into speakers of Ateso (the language of the Iteso) and those of the Karamojong cluster including the Turkana, Ikaramojong, Jie, and Dodoth in Kenya and Uganda.

Iteso traditions relate that the Iteso originated somewhere in what is now Sudan and moved south over a period of centuries. But it's not possible to calculate the time of this movement.

A body of Iteso is said to have separated from the Karamojong and moved further south. This may have been a very early separation because the clan names and ritual customs associated with the second of two distinctive groups of Karamojong and Jie people are not found among the Iteso.

Iteso clan names reveal a history of long-standing ethnic interactions. Names of Bantu and Northern Nilotic origin are found among them. And they were probably well-established in their northern Uganda heartland by the mid-1700s when they began to move farther south.

Traditions recorded among the JoPadhola indicate there were two waves of Iteso migration from what's now Sudan.

The first was family-based and peaceful. It was followed by a more extensive and aggressive migration that left the Iteso in control of a large swath of territory that by 1850 extended as far as the western highlands of Kenya.

European travellers record extensive fear of Iteso warriors; nonetheless, the Iteso soon suffered reverses that caused them to draw back to their current territory in Kenya.

Since then, the northern and southern Iteso territories have been separated.

Relations with other societies throughout the precolonial period were alternately peaceful and acrimonious.

And as a result of spatial inter-mixture and intermarriage, Iteso elements and customs can be found among neighbouring peoples and vice versa. Intermarriage has always been extensive.

It is likely that ethnic identity hardened during the colonial period, as it has since, when resources such as land were newly defined as belonging to "tribes."

The Iteso in Kenya and Uganda were conquered by African colonial agents of the British,And the colonial rulers ruled through them indirectly.

What's now western Kenya was transferred from Uganda to Kenya in 1902. As a result, the economic and political histories of the northern Iteso – those in Uganda – and the part of the southern Iteso living in Kenya have taken vastly different courses.

At independence, the Ugandan Iteso were far more wealthy than their Kenyan counterparts. This difference resulted from the status of Uganda as a protectorate reserved for "African development" and western Kenya's status as a labour reserve for the European-owned farms in the "White Highlands."

As a minority people in Kenya, the Iteso are not well-known and have been viewed with some suspicion by surrounding peoples. On the other hand, the Kenyan Iteso have not suffered from the political destabilisation their brethren have in Uganda since 1971 when Amin seized power.

Events in the colonial period and since have elaborated cultural differences among the Iteso that were regional in origin. The language of the northern Iteso, for example, was extensively influenced by the Baganda people, who ruled the Iteso on behalf of the British colonial regime, whereas that of the southern Iteso (in Kenya) is in some ways closer to Turkana.

As a result of living among Bantu- and Nilotic-speaking peoples, the southern Iteso have probably been subject to a greater variety of cultural influences.

The Teso territory in northeastern Uganda stretches south from Karamoja into the well-watered region of Lake Kyoga.

The great majority of Iteso occupy Soroti District and some of the adjacent areas in the north-eastern part of the country. Farther east and south, they constitute about half of the population of Bukedi District. These Iteso are separated from their more northern Ugandan colleagues by Bantu-speaking peoples, notably the Gisu, Banyole, and Bagwere.

They are not separated spatially from the Kenyan Iteso of Busia District in the Western Province, with whom they share a common border

The Iteso of Soroti District, Uganda, are called the northern Iteso in the ethnographic literature; the Iteso of Bukedi District, Uganda, and Busia District, Kenya, are called the southern Iteso.

The southern Iteso occupy the foothills of Mount Elgon and the surrounding savanna. The northern Iteso

164

environment varies from low and wet near the shores of Lake Kyoga and its neighboring swamps to high and arid in the north.

In both areas, annual rainfall is separated into two wet seasons – the "short" and "long" rains. It varies considerably from year to year and locality to locality.

The Iteso have always moved their households in response to changes in economy, politics, and climate. After the 1950s, land scarcity and colonial (later state) control prevented the Iteso from adapting their economy to the environment. And their population in the more arid parts of northern Uganda is sparse and small.

They're basically farmers but they also own cattle and other livestock. Originally they were cattle herders like the Karamojong but not strictly pastoralist.

Unlike the other Teso-speaking ethnic groups, the Iteso have never been transhumant or nomadic; agriculture has played as significant a role in their social, economic, and expressive lives as cattle have among the other groups. But recent cattle raids by the Karamojong – who use automatic weapons including AK 47s – have resulted in a sharp decline in cattle ownership among the Iteso.

In fact, the situation has deteriorated so badly in recent years that many people in the northern regions of the Teso territory have been forced to move to camps for displaced people fearing nigh-time raids by the Karamojong.

The civil strife intensified through the years especially since the mid-1980s. According to a report in the *New Scientist*, "Disease Stalks Villages in Uganda's Undeclared War":

"Three years of civil strife in Teso, northern Uganda, have forced half a million people from their homes and left another million starving and stricken by tuberculosis, snail fever (schistosomiasis), scabies and measles.

John Maitland, a British doctor who chairs the Teso Relief Committee and recently returned from a fact-

165

finding mission there, said that 'medical care, immunisation, planting and harvesting have all been reduced to nothing'.

Cattle rustlers from the Karamoja district have stolen five million animals from the Iteso - the inhabitants of Teso - in the three years since President Yoweri Museveni came to power in Uganda.

Museveni disarmed the Teso militia which protected the Iteso from raiders. The Iteso, who rely heavily on meat and milk, are now severely malnourished. They are caught between the disabling effects of their traditional enemy, the cattle raiders, and a disaffected guerrilla army.

The rebels raid Teso villages for food and money. According to Maitland, state health workers in Teso have run out of medicines and equipment: 'There is an alarming increase in schistosomiasis and tuberculosis. Measlea...is now a killer again.'

One of the most reputable hospitals in the region, Kumi Leprosy Hospital, is on the point of having to close altogether. The other four hospitals in the region are just running. 'AIDS is there just a little bit. It will increase because the soldiers are there,' Maitland says.

The Ministry of Relief and Social Rehabilitation has estimated that Soroti district needs 20 000 tonnes of maize and 14 000 tonnes of beans to plant, as well as 200,000 hoes, if it is to get a harvest this year." ("Disease Stalks Villages in Uganda's Undeclared War," *New Scientist*, 22 July 1989).

But the conflict in Teso territory in northeastern Uganda was not ignited by cattle rustling. It's true the Karamojong cattle rustlers unleashed terror among the Teso. However, the main culprit was a rebel group known as the Uganda People's Army.

It was based in Teso and started its insurgency against the government in 1987, about a year after Museveni seized power from President Obote. The group was

166

opposed to Museveni's rule and was active between 1987 and 1992.

It was also ethnic – mostly Teso and Nilotic, while most of the national leaders under Museveni were Bantu and southerners. Therefore the conflict also had an ethnic and regional dimension. The Teso supported Obote, a fellow Nilotic and fellow northerner.

The insurgency caused a lot of suffering among the Teso before it ended through mediation.

The Teso have been successful farmers for a long time unlike some of their neighbours. Even those who suffered during the war when their homeland was the battleground between the rebels and government forces have shown a remarkable degree of endurance. And many of them are successful farmers today as much as they were before the war.

One striking example was Winnie Asege who chaired a widows' organisation known as Dakabela Widows Farmers Association among the Teso. According to a report by Frederick Womakuyu in one of Uganda's leading newspapers, *New Vision*, in its edition of 2 March 2009, entitled "She Led Teso War Victims to the 'Promised Land'":

"She kept answering her phone as we drove on the dusty and uneven road to her home. We went past dry shrubs and grass-thatched huts before getting to her house, a permanent structure.

Winnie Asege, 38, of Dakabela village in Soroti district, is a successful farmer, who has inspired many in Teso region, eastern Uganda. But her journey has not been rosy.

Asege suffered extreme poverty, hunger, war and community bias against women, but she managed to pull through.

In 1987, the Uganda People's Army, a rebel group based in Teso, launched a struggle against the

Government. The women were mostly affected; many were raped and killed, but fortunately, some of them like Asege managed to escape.

'The rebels attacked our home at night and burnt two grass-thatched huts, but my husband and our child were hiding in a nearby bush. We had to walk through thick bushes for several days till we reached Karamoja. We were terrified by the several corpses we saw on our way.'

Asege did jobs like washing plates, till she raised enough money to start brewing malwa, a local brew. 'I couldn't do any other business apart from making local brew. But since I was getting wasted, I abandoned the business and returned home in the 1990s when the region was peaceful,' she says.

But on getting home, there was poverty and hunger. 'All our gardens had turned into bushes. There was virtually no crop – there was nothing to eat,' she says. 'Together with other women, we went back to cultivate our farms, but digging in bushy gardens was a task.'

Realising that it would take months or even years for one woman to plough a garden, she mobilised the Dakabela to form a group, to pull resources together and cultivate their fields.

'We formed a group of 10 women and set up a timetable. We ploughed each member's gardens in turns, until we finished the entire group's gardens,' she adds. 'We started by growing cassava on 10 acres.'

They sold the cassava at sh105,000. "We decided to continue growing cassava and also start growing cereal. Our earnings increased to about sh400,000," she adds. We named our group Dakabela Rural Women's Development Association. In 2001, when the group learnt that they were getting a raw deal from cereals, they went into citrus fruit growing.

'We had planted maize and had to wait for the next season to be able to grow more and besides, there was no income security. We also learnt that despite the fact that

168

citrus fruits do not mature quickly, they can be harvested two to three times a year,' Asege, the chairperson of the group, says.

'When we zeroed down on citrus fruits, the group acquired about eight acres of land for the project.'

They bought 400 trees of improved citrus fruits at sh2,000 per tree from the National Agricultural Research Organisation. They sold cassava and acquired a loan of sh1m to buy Valencia and Washington orange breeds.

In 2005, they harvested fruits on four acres. 'We managed to get about 284 bags because the weather was not good, but in 2006, we harvested 500 bags,' says Rose Alaso, a member of the group. 'We sold the fruits to our customers in Kenya at sh40,000 per bag. We also sold some in Rwanda, Kampala and Soroti.'

By 2006, the group had grown to about 35 members. More women joined the group due to the large profits it was making. 'We divided the money among ourselves. The National Agricultural Advisory Services (NAADS) was teaching farmers modern farming methods in Soroti, so we invited them to educate us' Alaso adds.

NAADS asked the group to identify a project in which to acquire more knowledge. 'Since we were already growing citrus fruits, we decided to concentrate on fruit growing,' Asege explains.

Armed with knowledge, they went back home and started individual projects. 'I set aside four acres of land for fruit growing. I bought about 400 seedlings from farmers in Soroti,' says Asege.

'My first harvest was last year. I got about 116 bags from two acres. I will harvest about 400 bags in December this year. I sell my fruits to Kenyans at sh50,000 a bag. I supplement my earnings with the group earning. In total, I make about sh20m annually.'

In 2006, the group planted more oranges, totalling to about 1,200. Each tree produces about two bags of oranges. 'Kenyans booked the fruits already and paid sh75,000 per tree. We made sh60m from the 800 trees,' she says.

The group also started a bee-keeping project. 'The NAADS sensitised us on bee-keeping and we learnt that it requires less labour,' Alaso says.

The NAADS and Italian Cooperazion, an NGO, gave the group four hives. From their fruit sales, they bought another 101 hives at sh50,000 each. Last year, the group harvested about 1,200kg of honey and sold each at sh6,000. 'We harvested honey from 30 hives. We hope to collect about 3,000 litres annually,' Asege says.

The group used its earnings from honey to start a piggery and goat keeping project. 'We bought six exotic pigs; two males and four females,' says Asege. 'We sold 10 piglets at sh20,000 each and acquired another six.'

The NAADS gave the women a hybrid he-goat to improve their breed. 'The project is still in infancy, but soon, we shall be able to sell one hybrid at sh150,000. A local breed costs sh40,000.' They group has about 40 local goats.

These projects have solved the groups' worries, as the members have been able to educate their children, access quality health care and live in decent houses.

'I make about sh20m from both my individual projects and the group investments. Three of my children are in good boarding schools in Kampala. I have also managed to build a house,' Asege says.

'I can afford to eat a balanced diet and will soon buy a vehicle,' she boasts.

At least six farmers in the group earn sh20m annually. Alaso makes sh4m annually. She is also constructing a permanent house.

During his recent visit to the region, President Yoweri Museveni visited the Dakabela association and pledged an irrigation pump. 'If the President fulfills his pledge, we shall be able to deal with the drought and cultivate more crops,' Asege says.

'We also don't have ready market; sometimes the price of a bag of oranges drops from sh40,000 to sh20,000,' Alaso says. 'The Government should find ready market for our products.'

The group is focusing on initiating new projects, like pineapple mango and pine growing." - (Frederick Womakuyu, "She Led Teso War Victims to the 'Promised Land,'" *New Vision*, Kampala, Uganda, 2 March 2009).

Many Tesos joined Uganda's cash economy when coffee and cotton were introduced in 1912 and the region has thrived through agriculture and commerce.

Traditionally, the Iteso lived in settlements consisting of scattered homesteads, each organized around a stockade and several granaries. And they still do so today, although with modernisation many also live independently while others have moved to urban centres in other parts of Uganda. They are urbanised like the Baganda, although not to the same extent.

Groups of homesteads are united around a hearth where men who form the core of the settlement gather for ritual and social purposes.

The groups usually consist of patrilineally related males whose wives, children and other relatives form the remainder of the settlement.

Several groups constitute a clan. Clans are loosely organised but clan elders maintain ritual observances in honour of their ancestors. However, such observances should not be construed as ancestor worship.

The Teso don't worship their departed ancestors but see them as intermediaries who intercede with God on their behalf; a common belief in many traditional African religions.

The Supreme Being is called *Edeke* in the Teso language.

Traditionally, the Teso believe that ancestral spirits bring bad luck if they are not appeased.

Every family had a shrine where libations were often poured or placed to placate the ancestors. And the practice is still common among many people who follow the traditional religion.

Western influence has had an impact in changing those beliefs. But even a significant number of people who have been converted to Christianity still believe in the power of their ancestors and their influence on the living.

Men of the clan consult the elders about social customs, especially marriage, and rituals.

Many of their customs are not unique in the region because of intermingling with members of other ethnic groups and shared history. The Teso share many cultural traits with the Langi, one of the largest ethnic groups in northern Uganda and in the country.

They have been influenced by the Karamojong who are their Nilotic brethren, and by Bantu groups especially the Basoga who, in turn, have been heavily influenced by the Baganda and the Banyoro.

There is also a clear division of labour in Teso society as is the case in many traditional societies in Uganda and other parts of Africa.

Much of the agricultural work is done by women. Women may also own land and granaries. But after the introduction of cash crops, most of the land was claimed by men and passed on to their sons.

Separation between men and women is also strictly enforced traditionally. Men and women don't eat together. They eat separately, a custom I have also observed among members of different ethnic groups including the Nyakyusa of southwestern Tanzania. Even modernised Africans from many different ethnic groups strictly enforce this custom, including those who live in cities.

The Teso also have strict taboos. Traditionally, women did not eat chicken the same way women didn't among the Toro.

There are a number of other animals even Teso men

were not allowed to eat. For example, the bush-buck –
called *ederet* in the Teso language – was taboo for many
clans.

It's still a male-dominated society and little has
changed in terms of relations between men and women in
spite of the influence of modernisation which has reached
even some of the most remote parts of Uganda in varying
degrees.

All Teso men within a settlement, related and
unrelated, are organised on the basis of age, similar to the
Nyakyusa of southwestern Tanzania whose age-villages
became the focus of some of the best anthropological
studies in Africa in the 1930s, especially by Professor
Monica Wilson of the School of African Studies at the
University of Cape Town.

She wrote about them in a number of books including
Good Company: A Study of Nyakyusa Age-Villages, and
Ritual and Kinship Among the Nyakyusa.

Tanzanian writer Godfrey Mwakikagile, who is a
Nyakyusa, has also written about them in his highly
acclaimed book *Africa and The West.*

And the role played by members of the age-villages
among the Nyakyusa is similar to the role played by their
counterparts among the Teso.

Each age-set among the Teso spans 15 to 20 years,
providing a generational framework for sharing the work
of the settlement. Age-sets also exercise social control by
recognising status distinctions based on seniority, both
between and within age groups. They also share
responsibility for resolving disputes within the settlement
or among neighbouring settlements, strikingly similar to
what the Nyakyusa did traditionally in southwestern
Tanzania.

The Teso are basically conservative and stick to
tradition probably more than many other groups in
Uganda. But also, like many other people of the Kenya-
Uganda border region, they have a history of extensive

173

multi-ethnic contact and have come to share many customs with neighbouring peoples, although not at the expense of their identity or cultural distinctiveness.

The Teso of Uganda have also been been described as being among the most economically adaptable of people. And in remarkable contrast, their brethren across the border in Kenya have an undeserved reputation for cultural conservatism. They are probably no more conservative than the Teso of Uganda.

Although all the major traditional kingdoms are located in southern Uganda, the northern part of the country is not without its share of attractions including major ethnic groups and traditional institutions.

Besides the Teso, the Acholi and the Langi are the other main groups in northern Uganda.

Strictly speaking, the Teso are a northeastern group, therefore still northern but not typical northern like the Acholi and the Langi.

The Langi are sometimes called Lango which is also the name of their language. They live in Lango, a sub-region in north-central Uganda north of Lake Kyoga.

Their language is a Luo language and is mutually intelligible with Acholi (which is also Luo) and is related to other Luo languages in Uganda and Kenya.

It's a western Nilotic language like those of the Acholi and the Alur who are their northern neighbours. But the Langi also share many cultural traits with the Ateker, their neighbours to the east and who are classified as eastern Nilotic.

When the Langi migrated to the region from the northeast – Sudan and some anthropologists claim from Ethiopia – they found the Acholi who had arrived there earlier, also from the north, and intermingled with them.

Because of their long interaction with the Acholi, the Langi lost their Ateker language and adopted Luo spoken by their Acholi neighbours.

The situation is similar to what happened in Ruanda-

174

Urundi (Rwanda and Burundi) where the Tutsi – who migrated from north – also lost their original language after intermingling with the Hutu and adopted the language of the people they had conquered.

In fact, in the case of Uganda, some Langis identify with the Luo.

But in spite of their linguistic affiliation with other Luo speakers, the vast majority of the Langi reject the "Luo" label. They say they're not Luo.

Some historians believe the Langi represent the descendants of 15th century dissenters from Karamojong society to the east.

Langi society is organised into localised patrilineages and further grouped into clans which are dispersed throughout the territory.

Clan members claim descent from a common ancestor. But they are seldom able to recount the nature of their relationship to the clan founder.

They have been well-organised as a society for centuries, although not as complex as the Bantu kingdoms of southern Uganda:

"(Traditionally), leadership was centered around the clan which would be both a kinship unit and the basic constituency of politics within the Rwotdoms.

The Rwot (chief) had the duty of controlling the entire clan. He was helped by a council of elders. The other senior members besides the Rwot were the leading elders of the clan.

The council of elders was responsible for the general administration and the maintenance of law and order within the clans. They organised the payment of debts, *luk* (adultery and fornication fines) as well as bride-wealth. Th(e) council was also responsible for the distribution or deposition of the property of the deceased.

Many clan elders were usually brought together to form the *Odonge-Atekere* and one of them would be

175

elected Rwot or *Awitong* as he was called.

The *Odongo-Atekere* were the clan branch leaders and the Rwot had the duty of controlling all the affairs of the clan. He led the warriors to war and mobilised defence during an invasion.

After battle, he organized a feast during which the *Moo* and *Moi* (military ranks) were conferred upon those that deserved them. These ranks were for those who had displayed excellent performances during the battle.

Dwelling

The Langi dwelt in villages. A village could contain more than a hundred huts built in a line. In front of the hut, there was a line of granaries belonging to the individual families. Beyond them, at a distance, was the community cattle kraal.

When someone needed a new site on which to build a hut, he would take a chicken and some beer to the desired site and leave them there for a day or two. If on his return he found that something had eaten the chicken or drunk the beer, he would abandon the site as it was considered an ill-omen.

For fear of evil spirits, the Langi avoided building near swamps and also avoided building near stony or rocky ground.

The huts were of different types. An *iguruguru* was a small hut intended for sleeping in as a guest house. It was made with a low doorway that people had to enter crawling.

The low doorway was to prevent enemies from aiming their spears at the people sleeping during the night.

The unmarried youths slept in small huts called *otogo* whose doorways, approached by means of a ladder, were only big enough to allow a person to craw in and out.

This type of hut is now very rare but it had its entrance closed by a grass mat and is said to have been very warm inside.

The family shrine (Abila)

It was built in front of the home and it was identified by particular plants.

The shrine had a great degree of sacredness surrounding it. It was not only a resting place for the ancestral spirits but it was a place where spears were blessed before and after the hunt.

All skulls of the animals which were killed during the hunt were placed at the Abila and, except for the very elderly; women were forbidden from changing anything placed in the Abila.

Military

The society had no standing army. All able-bodied men were considered warriors.

Before war could be declared, a foreteller would be consulted to predict the results of the war. If luck was 'proved,' old women would spit into the hands of the warriors and they would then set off. The leaves of the *olwedo* tree were put in the path where the warriors passed to enhance their luck in the impending fight.

War booty was normally retained by whoever looted it. After the war, a ceremony was convened in which to award the *Moi* ranks. The person who killed a big or an important person was styled *Anuk*; his privileges and other titles were increased by making tattoo marks on his left shoulder and neck.

The highest *Moi* was *Abwangor*. During this ceremony, a goat was slaughtered while the elders stood in front of the family shrine and its blood was allowed to drip on the warriors. The goat was then skinned and its meat divided accordingly.

Judicial system

The judicial system of the Langi was harsh by modern standards because in certain instances, offenders could be dealt with on the spot by whoever caught them. For instance, there was no case to answer if a man speared another one to death after having found him sleeping with his wife.

There was nothing like manslaughter since a murderer would be killed if he was caught. So also could a notorious thief. As for the latter, he could even be killed by his own people.

Often on the intervention of elders, murder could be compensated in the form of goats, cows or a young girl. If the murdered person was a man and the girl who would be surrendered gave birth to a boy, she would be set free and returned to her people.

If she had proved good, she would be married to a young man within the clan and bride wealth would be accordingly paid.

Murder victims were almost always men since it was considered cowardly to kill a woman or a child.

If a woman killed her husband, she would be returned to her people and the bride wealth would be refunded. She would in addition be required to pay compensation.

The woman had a lesser role than a man to play in society except as a source of wealth and custodian of the rituals of birth divination.

Other offences in the Lango society included pre-marital pregnancies and fornication. If a boy refused to marry a girl and the girl died in labour, the case was tantamount to murder. If she successfully delivered, the child would remain property of the girl's parents and could only be redeemed if the boy married the girl.

Wizards were usually held responsible for causing deaths, the failure of crops, long periods of drought and other devilish acts against society. Such wizards whenever caught or proven were executed.

Proof in such cases was always arbitrary.

Part of such proof was the possession of odd objects whose purpose was completely unknown to the people, for example, the placenta of a new born baby or the bones of a dead person." - ("The Langi of Uganda: Origin, Religion and Culture, Dwelling, Political Set-up").

Originally, the Langi were pastoralists but they later became farmers.

They ate meat and drank milk. And their economy was based on barter. They used to barter cattle, goats and grains with the Acholi, the Labwor, and the Kumam and later, with the Arabs. But as they continued to move towards Lake Kyoga, they abandoned their pastoral economy.

But they still own livestock. So they are both "pastoral" and agricultural – except that they now live in permanent settlements instead of moving from place to place as typical pastoralists do, traversing vast expanses of territory in search of pasture.

Their main crop is millet. They also rely on animal husbandry for subsistence. In some areas, people also cultivate maize, eleusine, peanuts, sesame seed, sweet potatoes, and cassava.

They also grow and eat simsim which was introduced by the colonial government in 1911.

When they first started farming, their first food crops were millet, peas and others. They later started to grow groundnuts and sweet potatoes which were introduced form Bunyoro.

Both Langi and Acholi generally assign agricultural tasks either to men or women. In many cases, men are responsible for cattle while women work in the fields.

In some villages, only adult men may milk cows.

An Acholi or Langi man may marry more than one

wife, but he may not marry within his lineage or that of his mother. A woman lives in her husband's homestead which may include his brothers and their families. Each wife has a separate house and hearth for cooking.

Many of these cultural practices and customs are shared by other Nilotic groups in northern Uganda, although some of them are unique to the Langi.

The Langi have also been victims of violence for decades since Idi Amin rose to power in January 1971. Although some of them initially supported him as a fellow northerner, they later fell out of favour with him as did the Acholi.

The majority of the Langi and the Acholi in the army did not support Amin; they supported Obote.

Also, Amin was not a Langi or an Acholi. He was a Kakwa, a member of one of the smallest ethnic groups in Uganda.

And, although he was a northerner, he did not come from the same region as the Langi and the Acholi did in north-central Uganda. He came from West Nile, a region in the far northwest bordering Congo and Sudan.

During Obote's return to the presidency in 1980, the Acholi did not support him as they did in the past when he was Uganda's leader from the 1960s until his ouster by Amin in 1971. They accused him of favouring his fellow Langis at the expense of the Acholi. As Thomas P. Ofcansky states in his book *Uganda: Tarnished Pearl of Africa*:

"Since late 1984, Vice-President and Defense Minister Paulo Muwanga (a Muganda from Buganda) had been plotting against Obote.

Apart from objecting to the president's plan to name his cousin, Akena Adoko, chairman of the Public Service Commission, Muwanga wanted to negotiate with the insurgents – unlike Obote, who believed he could achieve military victory over his opponents.

180

Although these differences slowly weakened his regime, Obote lost power because of his inability to preserve the fragile Langi-Acholi alliance, especially in the UNLA (Uganda National Liberation Army).

Many Acholi believed that Obote favored his fellow Langi in new military appointments and promotions.

In August 1984, this conflict escalated when Obote named Smith Opon-Acak, a Langi, to the post of chief of staff. This left the soon-to-retire seventy-one-year-old General Tito Lutwa Okello as the only Acholi in a key military position.

As soon as Opon-Acak tok office, Acholi personnel accused him of unfairly advancing the careers of his fellow Langi and of deploying only Acholi troops to combat zones.

Soon afterward, disaffected Acholi soldiers started plotting with opposition leaders to overthrow Obote. Troops in the ranks also began disobeying their Langi officers. In June 1985, for example, soldiers assigned to Magamaga Ordnance Depot refused to go into combat against the NRA – Museveni's National Resistance Army – in western Uganda.

A few weeks later, inter-ethnic fighting at Mbuya Barracks, which came about when it became known that Obote had ordered the arrest of several Acholi officers, claimed the lives of at least thirty UNLA personnel.

To prevent a future purge or massacre of Acholi military personnel, Brigadier Basilio Okello, an Acholi, mobilized anti-government UNLA troops at his Gulu headquarters (in Acholiland in northern Uganda) and marched on Kampala to overthrow Obote.

Along the way, he defeated pro-Obote Langi forces at Karuma Falls and at Bombo (Bombo was the headquarters of the Ugandan army and the Ministry of Defence until December 2007 when they were moved to Mbuya, a suburb of Kampala).

Finally, on 27 July 1985, Brigadier Basilio Okello and

his men entered Kampala, seized Radio Uganda, and announced that Obote's regime had come to an end." - (Thomas P. Ofcansky, *Uganda: Tarnished Pearl of Africa*, Westview Press, Boulder, Colorado, USA, 1999, p. 56. See also Phares Mukasa Mutibwa, *Uganda Since Independence: A Story of Unfulfilled Hopes*, Africa World Press, Lawrenceville, New Jersey, USA, 1992).

Obote's reliance on his fellow Langis in the government and in the military as well as intelligence services could, ostensibly, be attributed to concern for security – as some may contend – since he could not trust members of other ethnic groups.

In Ghana, for example, Jerry Rawlings was accused of having given a disproportionately large number of high government posts – including intelligence – to Ewes from the Volta Region in eastern Ghana. His mother was an Ewe and his father Scottish.

Security was one of the major reasons given for favouring members of his tribe. Supporters of Obote gave the same reason.

There's some truth to that. And most African leaders advance the same argument.

But in most cases, it's raw-naked tribalism by these leaders. And it has almost ruined Africa, igniting conflicts in different parts of the continent.

Whether or not Obote had genuine fear of members of other ethnic groups whom he thought might overthrow him is besides the point. What's critical is that the appointment of a disproportionately large number of his fellow tribesmen, the Langi, to high positions in the government and in the military infuriated and alienated many people who were not Langi.

And that was potential for catastrophe in the context of Uganda's volatile politics and ethnic relations. As Professor Phares Mukasa Mutibwa, a Muganda, of Makerere University states in his book *Uganda Since*

Independence: A Story of Unfulfilled Promises:

"Within the military the Acholis Tito Okello, the Army Commander, and Bazilio Okello, commander of 10 Brigade Northern Zone, based in Gulu, also felt that the time had come to negotiate with the NRA fighters.

For the Acholi soldiers, who formed the bulk of the army, the war which Museveni's guerrillas were fighting against Obote was quickly becoming a war against the Acholis only.

The soldiers who were being sent to the war front were virtually all Acholi, and the Langi officers and men were manning safe areas of Kampala and being deliberately kept away from the war zones.

In short, those who were dying in hundreds to prop up Obote's fledgling regime were not Langis but Acholis.

Thus Acholis' concern over Obote's determination to continue the war against Museveni was less humanitarian than due to the realisation that if the war did not stop, their sons would continue to die at the hands of the NRA. They joined the negotiation lobby to save their skins, and thus in Obote's eyes they became a disloyal group – marked men....

It became obvious to all that Obote was ignoring the Acholi factor in the Acholi-Langi alliance on which the fortunes of the 'liberators' group of the UPC (Obote's Uganda People's Congress) had depended since Amin's overthrow.

The Acholi began to see that Obote was pursuing a deliberate policy of discriminating against them in favour of his own tribe, the Langi. It was the time-honoured game of using allies to get into power and dumping them when he could use them no longer." - (Phares Mukasa Mutibwa, *Uganda Since Independence: A Story of Unfulfilled Hopes*, op.cit., pp. 161, and 162).

Ethnicity became the paramount factor virtually in all

appointments. And Obote continued to pile up enemies. He had the Langi on his side. But everything else was stacked against him. As Professor Mutibwa goes on to say:

"It was not only in the civil service and the management of the economy that the Langis were taking the lion's share. In the military too they were being pushed into positions which others thought they did not merit.

The most celebrated example of this development came when the Army Chief of Staff, (Major-General) David Oyite-Ojok, was killed when his helicopter was shot down by the NRA at Kasuzi near Nakasongola in December 1983.

All eyes were focused on Obote to see whom he would nominate for this crucial post.

Did he have a Langi to put in the shoes of his long-time comrade-in-arms and confidant, Oyite-Ojok?

All those best qualified to replace Oyite-Ojok, most notably Bazilio Okello, were Acholi.

Obote mused to himself. He did not have a suitable Langi for the post, but after postponing the decision for almost six months, he appointed Smith Opon-Acak (a Langi)....

By the beginning of 1985 Obote was not in control of what was going on in Uganda generally, but especially in the field of the military which was clearly in the hands of the aggrieved Acholis.

In June 1985, at the crucial moment when his personal presence at the scene of events was of paramount importance, Obote left the capital to officiate at a not very important ceremony at Mbale – one is reminded of his trip to Singapore in January 1971, leaving the road clear for the coup by Idi Amin.

Oblivious of the true significance of his enemies' plans and actions, Obote started issuing orders and sending emissaries from Mbale.

He directed his lieutenants in Kampala to take charge

of the situation, and to arrest and detain the associates of Brigadier Okello. He sent an emissary – a Mr. Wacha-Olal, who had acted as one of the members of the presidential triumvirate during the time of the Military Commission in 1980 – with proposals for peace-talks to Bazilio Okello, then in Gulu, but the Acholi brigadier was no longer interested in such proposals from a man whom he could not trust.

Instead, Bazilio Okello sent a message to the north across the border with Southern Sudan where the supporters of Amin and former soldiers of the FUNA (under Major-General Lumago) were living.

An agreement was concluded between the Acholi and the West Nile FUNA (Former Uganda National Army) remnants, on th basis of which an Acholi-West Nile alliance was established to collaborate in Obote's overthrow.

The FUNA fighters and other West Nile elements arrived in Kampala a few days before the coup.

As everything was collapsing all around him, Obote made a last desperate appeal to his 'godfather,' Julius Nyerere, to send troops to quell the Acholi coup, but Julius did not act.

Perhaps he had had enough enough of Uganda's problems, and in any case Nyerere, with his *Ujamaa* policies in tatters, was in the process of packing his own bags to make way for his successor, Ndugu Ali H. Mwinyi.

Nyerere told Obote that as he was soon leaving office he could not commit his successor to policies which would in effect be open-ended.

Many Ugandans sighed with relief, to see that at last the great Tanzanian leader had realised the folly of endlessly propping up a man, however close a friend he might be, who was so unpopular in his own country.

Tanzania's policies towards Obote and his government had in fact begun to shift from as early as mid-1984 – to the extent that it started quietly supporting the NRA's fight against Obote.

While his UPC parliamentarians were waiting in the National Assembly for the start of a meeting which he himself had summoned, Obote boarded his Mercedes and drove towards the Kenyan border.

This time he overflew Tanzania on his way to Zambia. His regime was over." - (Ibid., pp. 162, 164 – 165).

Obote, a Langi, was gone. He never again regained power and died 20 years later on 10 October 2005 at the age of 80.

But when General Tito Lutwa Okello, an Acholi, became head of state after Obote's ouster, the ruling Military Council which was the government was predominantly Acholi. Five of the nine Military Council members were Acholi.

It was a clear-cut case of ethnic favouritism. It was also one of the main reasons why Museveni's National Resistance Movement (NRM) refused to join the government of "national unity" although other opposition groups did.

Still, the ouster of Obote did not end suffering for the Acholi. They had suffered under Amin, and they were to suffer again.

It was also just the beginning for the Langi – at least the second phase. They had been favoured under Obote. So they did not suffer under his rule. But, like the Acholi, they also suffered earlier under Idi Amin. And they were to suffer again together with the Acholi.

Both – the Langi and the Acholi – have suffered at the hands of the Lord's Resistance Army (LRA), a rebel group which has been wreaking havoc across northern Uganda for more than 20 years.

The terror unleashed by the Lord's Resistance Army has sometimes degenerated into inter-ethnic violence between the Acholi and the Langi in northern Uganda:

186

"The massacre of more than 200 people last Saturday by Lords Resistance Army (LRA) rebels in a displaced people's camp in the Lira district (in Langi territory) has culminated in inter-ethnic violence, leaving five people dead.

The ethnic killings took place in Lira town Wednesday afternoon during a protest demonstration organized against the Saturday massacre of civilians. It is the first time ethnic violence between the Langi and Acholi tribes has erupted in the 18-year rebellion in northern Uganda.

The two ethnic tribes share the same language and many cultural norms and have also borne the brunt of LRA attacks. But the Langi are blaming the Acholi for allegedly forming the bulk of the LRA, whose leader Joseph Kony is from the Acholi tribe.

Hundreds of Acholi and Langi have either been killed or abducted by the LRA. One of the worst massacres, in which more than 240 people were killed by the LRA, took place in Atiak in Acholi land in 1995.

The peaceful protest demonstration degenerated into the indigenous Langi attacking the Acholi living in Lira town, killing five. The Acholi are located in the Gulu, Kitgum and Pader districts, while the Langi are in the neighboring Lango district.

The demonstration, planned to protest the attack on the Barlonyo internally displaced people's camp, saw police shoot dead two other people when the crowd attacked a police station accusing them of failure to provide security.

Mobs ran wild and set fire to several homes and restaurants thought to belong to Acholi people. Some Acholi are now taking refuge at Lira police station, while many others are in hiding.

Some of the demonstrators held banners reading 'The United Nations must intervene' or 'Stop political pride and seek foreign military assistance.' The banners were referring to the war in northern Uganda which has claimed thousands of lives.

The Ugandan government of President Yoweri Museveni continues to reject requests from opposition politicians and church leaders to seek foreign assistance to end the war, maintaining it will defeat the rebels militarily.

Many politicians and church leaders have condemned the inter-ethnic violence development between the two tribes, with Gulu Diocese Archbishop John Baptist Odama saying, 'We have been very saddened by the recent events in northern Uganda. Today a peace march ends up in a death trap.'

A member of parliament for Lira municipality, Cecilia Ogwal, criticized President Museveni for what she said is responsibility for continuation of the war.

'Have a compassionate heart toward northern Uganda just like you have for western and other parts of Uganda.'

He seems to have this 'I don't care' attitude because that is why the war has lasted for 18 years. Please treat us like the rest of Uganda,' she said." - (Report from Lira, northern Uganda, "Inter-ethnic Violence Follows Massacre in Northern Uganda," published in *Asian Political News*, Kyodo News International, Inc., 26 February, 2004).

The people of northern Uganda have suffered on an unprecedented scale.

And it's ironic that both – the Langi and the Acholi – have been victims of violence unleashed by fellow northerners, starting with Amin. As Jenkins Kiwanuka, a retired high-ranking government official who worked in Uganda's ministry of foreign affairs, stated in his report in *The Monitor*, Kampala, Uganda, in its edition of 2 February 2008, entitled "There Was No Harmony Between Amin and Langi After Obote's Overthrow":

"Samuel Olara, a human rights advocate and son of dictator Idi Amin's one time comrade-in-arms, the late Gen. Bazilio Olara Okello, took advantage of the 37th

Anniversary of the coup that propelled Amin to power to join the numerous writers who have testified to the killing of thousands of Langi and Acholi soldiers and ordinary Ugandans during Amin's regime.

In his article 'Amin's Dead and the Game of Numbers' (*Daily Monitor*, January 26 and *Sunday Minitor*, 27 Jan), Olara talked about 'some attempts' that had been made in the media 'to whitewash the Amin regime.'

He was obviously referring to columnist Timothy Kalyegira's desperate defence of Amin last year when he challenged the people of Uganda to give him at least 600 names of people who were allegedly murdered by Amin.

Unfortunately, or possibly fortunately for Kalyegira, his crusade was brought to an abrupt end by a public that detested his defence of Amin's horrors.

And as if that was not enough, Okello's own son now comes out and condemns Amin.

I am personally happy though, because Olara has given me yet another opportunity to correct the misrepresentations Kalyegira made in his article titled 'Amin's Dealings with Acholi, Langi in the 70s' (*Daily Monitor*, November 10, 2007).

He said in that article that after Obote's ouster, the dictator maintained 'harmonious working relations' with soldiers and public servants from the two tribes; that 'many of Amin's inner circle bodyguards from 1971 to 1979' were Acholi and Langi. He also made the point that even Amin's first wife was a Langi; that from 1965 Amin had a Langi personal secretary called Rose Akullo, who died in a motor accident in 1977.

First of all, Amin had a Langi wife in 1954. I wrote about her long ago and told how Amin returned to his house at Jinja army barracks and found former President Obote's cousin, the late Dan Albert Obote (a Langi), and another man talking to her.

When they could not tell him what they were doing in his house during his absence, he held them by the neck

189

and, in their own words, banged their foreheads against each other rhythmically, 'as if he was playing an accordion'.

When he released them, they fled to my house, which was nearby, and I administered first aid to them.

Like Amin, Obote also married a Muganda wife, Miria Kalule, but that did not stop him from sending his troops to Luwero where thousands of Baganda were killed during his war against the National Resistance Movement, or from attacking the Kabaka of Buganda's palace.

Miriam (also known as Miria) herself confessed in an interview that whenever she tried to talk to her husband about what was going on, Obote would retort that they (the UPC – Uganda People's Congress – government) knew what they were doing.

I first met Amin in 1954 in the army at Jinja, so I knew him well enough. Because he was a brave soldier, he was very popular among his fellow soldiers all of whom, like him, were non-commissioned. They included Acholis and Langis.

Amin used as window dressing the Acholis like Pangarasio Onek, the bandmasters, bodyguards and chaplains who stayed in the army after he took power. They were not a threat to him at all. In any case, they were kept under constant surveillance by intelligence agencies and spies from the other tribes Amin trusted, and so were those in the civil service.

Why, if Amin still trusted the Acholis and Langis as Kalyegira alleged, did he order the Acholi bodyguard out of his vehicle while he was driving some journalists around the bazooka-shelled section of Entebbe airport?

Olara's testimony renders added credibility to what Apollo Lawoko stated in his *Dungeons of Nakasero* that Amin at one time devised a plan, that later aborted, to reduce the population of the Acholis and Langis by 25 percent.

Amin could promote you today and have you

'removed' the next day. He once directed a Col. Arube to inspect a guard of honour in Entebbe in his presence (I was personally there), only to hear a few days later that Arube had been murdered. It was alleged that that he had been plotting to stage a coup.

The same Amin once called me and the then Foreign Minister, Elizabeth Bagaya, to his office and branded us saboteurs for informing our embassies of a statement he had himself issued accusing members of the Langi and Acholi communities in Nakawa and Naguru of sharpening spears and pangas to destabilise the country.

He ordered that they be kept under surveillance and directed Radio Uganda to broadcast the statement continuously, attributing it first to a government spokesman, then to a police spokesman, then to an army spokesman and finally to a 'public spokesman.'

When a Military Attach'e in Moscow, an Acholi, protested against the surveillance, Amin denied any knowledge of the statement and assured the officer that those were fabrications from the Ministry of Foreign Affairs.

That is the situation that Kalyegira described as 'harmonious relations' between Amin and the Langis and Acholis, and if indeed they were, then I am afraid the expression has lost its meaning."

The Langi were not safe under Amin, although initially some people thought they were because they and Amin were fellow northerners, even if from different regions in the north.

Being from far northwest, Amin was not really a typical northerner like Obote.

And the most prominent ethnic group in northern Uganda is not the Langi but the Acholi. The Langi are second to the Acholi in terms of prominence in northern Uganda.

The Acholi are also one of the most well-known ethnic

191

groups in Uganda and in the entire East Africa.

They speak Luo as their native language.

Their homeland is the former Acholi District – now divided into the Gulu and Kitgum districts – and the adjoining area of southern Sudan. Most of them live in Uganda.

The Acholi landscape is characterised by rolling grasslands with scattered trees, streams, and rock outcrops. Northern Uganda is usually drier and less fertile than the south. The dry season is long and hot and the Acholi have adapted to this harsh environment.

Most Acholis are farmers – or peasants. Their man crops include millet, sorghum,beans, various kinds of peas, maize, cassava, vegetables, groundnuts, simsim (sesame), fruits and cotton.

The most common domestic animals are – and have long been – chickens and goats, with some cattle, especially in the dryer portions of Acholi.

Men have traditionally played a significant role in agriculture, especially for such time-limited, labour-intensive tasks as clearing, planting, and harvesting, often as part of lineage-based cooperative labour teams.

Women also work in the fields. They're also responsible for most child rearing, all cooking and other food-preparation tasks.

The building of houses and granaries has historically involved both men and women, with each performing specified functions.

Boys and girls are typically socialised into distinct gender roles and do household and other chores accordingly.

Since the advent of colonial rule, an average of 10 to 20 per cent of adult Acholi males at any one time have been involved in migrant labour or employment in the police or army that has taken them from their home and families – mostly to the south.

But only a small number of Acholis have filled middle-level or senior civil-service positions in independent Uganda. Most of these jobs are taken by southerners who are, relatively speaking, far more educated than their northern counterparts.

The situation is reminiscent of what happened in Nigeria where northerners – especially the Hausa – also joined the army during colonial rule and after independence in disproportionately large numbers as riflemen, while better educated southerners, mostly Ibgos and the Yorubas, served as army officers and as civil servants.

The neighbours of the Acholi include the Luo-speaking Langi, Paluo, and Alur to the south and southwest, the central Sudanic-speaking Madi to the west, and the eastern Nilotic Jie and Karamojong to the east.

One of the main reasons why the Acholi are so prominent in Ugandan contemporary history is that they joined the army in very large numbers and virtually dominated the armed forces as did other northerners.

Although the Acholi constituted less than 5 per cent of Uganda's population during the early years of independence, they were disproportionately represented in the army. An entire third of the enlisted men in the Ugandan army were Acholi. And more than 15 per cent of the police force were also Acholi.

Their dominant role in the armed forces also enabled them to play a major role in Uganda's political life.

When Obote first became prime minister and then president, they strongly supported him as a fellow northerner although he was a Langi, not an Acholi. And when Idi Amin seized power, they also supported him against his southern opponents.

And the military rulers of Uganda after Amin was overthrown were Acholi and other northerners until a southerner, Yoweri Museveni, rose to power after he toppled Obote.

Museveni became the first southerner, and the first

Bantu, since independence to lead Uganda on long term-basis, besides Benedicto Kiwanuka who served very briefly as prime minister a few months before independence and Yusuf Lule who served as president, also for a very short period of time, after Amin was overthrown. The rest were Nilotic, and from northern Uganda.

General Tito Okello, an Acholi, was president of Uganda for six months from 1985 until January 1986 when he was ousted by Museveni. And another Acholi, Bazilio Olara-Okello, also briefly served as Uganda's military head of state for two days between 27 and 29 July 1985 when he was chairman of the military council, the supreme ruling body during that tumultuous period. He later became lieutenant-general and chief of the armed forces.

Even the army officers were mainly Acholi, as were the enlisted men, during those years. And they recruited into their ranks fellow northerners including the Langi, members of President Obote's ethnic group.

But their prominence in Uganda's security forces – army, intelligence, and air force – has also been a curse, sometimes, in a country wracked by violence. The violence has been fuelled by ethnic rivalries and the Acholi have been at the centre of this maelstrom in a number of conflicts.

In the most recent phase of conflict beginning in the mid-1980s, the Acholi have largely been at the receiving end of the violence. Uganda's current army, various local rebel groups and heavily armed Karamojong raiders have all raped, looted, killed, and destroyed, making any kind of normal life in Acholiland impossible.

Traditionally, the Acholi have been ruled by chiefs for centuries. Chiefdoms consisted of a number of fenced villages, each with recognised land rights vested in the patrilineal lineage – known as *kaka* – at its core.

Lineage heads, assisted by lineage elders, organised

production based on cooperative village-lineage labour; controlled marriage; oversaw rituals and were the main advisors to the chief. They were also responsible for most of the social control exercised in Acholi.

But through the decades, chiefdoms in Acholi have become vestigial institutions, and the fences that once enclosed villages have disappeared.

Most Acholi, however, continue to live in neighbourhoods – parishes – that not only consist predominantly of patrilineal kinsmen and their wives but often carry the old lineage names.

Most Acholi also continue to live in thatched, round mud houses, although wealthier ones and those who live in towns or near major roads have square houses of mud or block with iron or tile roofs.

Localised patrilineal lineages, some of which have "brother" lineages of the same or different name in other parts of Acholi, have long been the fundamental social and economic units in Acholi.

Numbering between 400 and 500 by the turn of the 20th century, these exogamous groups claim descent from a common ancestor – although means exist to incorporate many types of "outsiders" as well – and have special lineage shrines, ritual ceremonies, praise-calls and totems.

Traditional religion still plays a very important role in the lives of many Acholis.

Historically, Acholi religious beliefs focused on three types of spirits. There were the spirits of known relatives, especially lineage ancestors. The second type was non-ancestral and was for the chiefdom as a whole.

Spirits of both of these types were generally beneficent. They were approached with such general concerns as good health, fertility, and appeals or thanks for good harvests in ceremonies that usually emphasised the consciousness, cohesiveness, and continuation of their respective groups as functioning corporate entities.

The third group of spirits were those of unknown

persons and dangerous beasts. These were hostile and personified as ghosts and were believed to cause sickness and other misfortunes and were dealt with by means of spirit possession.

Extensive mission activity in Acholiland by both Protestants and Catholics has attracted many followers since the second decade of the 20th century, bringing about fundamental change in the lives of many people in that part of Uganda.

But in spite of all that, traditional beliefs still persist and are often meshed with Christian doctrine in complex ways. One illustration of this is the various spirit-possession-based millennial – and military – movements that have been prominent in Acholi during the extremely difficult period of the late 1980s and early 1990s, most famously the Holy Spirit Movement of Alice Lakwena.

The Lord's Resistance Army (LRA) led by John Kony, a cousin of the late Alice Lakwena, is the most brutal manifestation of these kinds of religious beliefs which are also expressed by military means. Kony claims he speaks with angels and wants Uganda to be ruled on the basis of the Ten Commandments.

Ironically, he's an Acholi himself who has unleashed terror and wreaked havoc among his own people for more than two decades and continues to do so at this writing in 2009.

His rebel group has been responsible for tens of thousands of deaths through the years since he launched his rebellion in 1986 when Museveni came to power. And the Acholi are among those who have suffered the most in this brutal conflict.

Tens of thousands more have been enslaved and raped and have had their limbs, lips and ears chopped off by the LRA rebels. Countless of these victims have been children who have been forcibly recruited to serve in the Lord's Resistance Army as child soldiers, porters and as sex slaves. And the rebels continue to wreak havoc in northern

Uganda with impunity. It is a horrendous tragedy.

The suffering is unparalleled in the history of Uganda, the misery and horror seldom seen elsewhere, telescoped in this collective sentiment echoed by the victims: "When the sun sets, we start to worry."

It's time to go to refugee camps where it's safe to sleep. And it's not always safe, because of the rebels. They could strike anytime. And they have, many times.

It's living hell.

Although the Lord's Resistance Army is responsible for this carnage, others are equally responsible.

The rebels don't make weapons. They don't make guns. They don't make bullets. Someone is arming them.

Sudan has been known to provide them with weapons and operational bases for years. But there are others. Some army officers within the Ugandan army itself are also responsible for fuelling and perpetuating the conflict.

And others place the blame even farther afield, across oceans. Although there's some truth to that – without the weapons which are manufactured abroad and which are sold to rebel groups in Africa, there would be no atrocities perpetrated on this scale – it would be wrong to blame outsiders for the entire holocaust, a calamity that has now become synonymous with northern Uganda.